ASHLEY W. GILLETTE

RED

FLAGS

RUN

THE WARNING SIGNS IN
RELATIONSHIPS

ISBN 978-0-9987200-2-9
Keen Vision Publishing, LLC
www.keen-vision.com

In Loving Memory of

FANTASIA WILLIAMS

You were a sweet young lady whose smile could brighten up a room. Rest in peace, Fantasia.

ACKNOWLEDGEMENTS

First and foremost, I give praise and honor to God, the Creator of my life. You have made it clearer than ever that You have me in Your hands. You told me to FINISH and here it is. THANK YOU!

I am grateful for my mother, Carolyn T. Gillett, who covers me in prayer and is always quick to tell everyone who already knows it that I'm her daughter. Mommy, I love you to life. Thank you for everything you do and continue to do for me!

I am a daddy's girl. Elmer L. Gillett, the world's most amazing father, makes it hard for me not to be. Daddy, thank you for protecting me, covering me, and so much more. You are my first love. I love you to life. Thank you for everything.

I have the best big sister a girl could ask for. Maritza Walton, thank you for guiding me, investing in my vision and always being there when I need you. You taught me about true praise and worship and you keep me on my toes every single day. I love you to life, lady. Thank you for being such a blessing to my life.

To my close friend, Jessica D. Price, creator of Je'Dan Couture. Thank you for believing in me, praying for me, and helping me daily. Thank you for all you have done.

I would like to thank Jessica D. Williams of Keen Vision Publishing for helping me to get these words out to the world. Words can't express how much your belief in me has helped me. Thank you for answering my crazy text messages any time of the day or night. Thank you for getting on to me when I wanted to say forget it. Everything happens for a reason, and I have truly been blessed by my divine connection to you and your vision.

Special thanks to all my friends and family who stood by and checked on me daily. I LOVE YOU!

Finally, to you, the reader. Thank you for your support!

Love,

Ashley

ABOUT THE AUTHOR

Ashley W. Gillett is the vice president of Executive Suittee Professional Women's Network. She is a leader who has vowed to provide women with the resources and tools needed to take control of their lives. Her passion is to help guide people out of dead-end relationships and to discover their self-worth.

Ashley has a heart for others, and is a natural leader. She takes pleasure in hosting vision board parties, retreats, and workshops to equip budding entrepreneurs or those making a commitment to having healthy lifestyles. As a worship leader, she oversees and trains the worship team at Community Worship Center Church of the Nazarene in Brooklyn, NY. She has served in this position for ten years under the leadership of her father and senior pastor, Dr. Elmer L. Gillett.

She is currently in the process of recording a short worship album. This album will encourage intimate prayer time with God. Ashley enjoys spending quality time with her friends and family. One of her greatest passions is to positively influence the goals and growth of her family and friends.

CONTENTS

INTRODUCTION 1

Part One: Red Flags in Relationships

THE "BABY BOY" 3

THE DERANGED MAN 15

THE PLAYBOY 33

THE LIAR 47

THE BROKE MAN 81

Part Two: Red Flags in Dating

THE DEACON 99

THE CONVICT 111

THE DIVA 123

THE MUTE 135

Part Three: Self-Reflection

Red Flags Run 147

STAY CONNECTED 149

INTRODUCTION

In this book, I will transparently share many of the relationships I've dealt with on my journey of finding out my value. I was raised in a great family, with both my mother and father who are still happily married. However, I got involved in some relationships that I knew didn't match up with what they taught me.

The lessons I've learned about relationships came at the cost of me bumping my head really hard. In most of the relationships, I saw the warning signs early on but still refused to run away. As a result, I wasted a lot of money, cried many tears, and lost so much time. I had a *type* as we all do. Over time, I realized that the *type* I fell for always left me brokenhearted. My goal is to ensure that you don't have to experience that.

Now, I am a single woman with no rush to be in a relationship. Even though it gets a little lonely sometimes, I would rather wait for the man God has for me, than to run the risk of having my heart broken by some random joker.

Though the stories may be hilarious, they are very real. I want you to get a good laugh, but don't overlook the message behind each story. It is time out for settling for mediocrity and nonsense in relationships. What many of us fail to realize is that the time we spend in dead end relationships could be used to do something great and productive. Believe it or not, relationships require a lot of time and energy. Bad relationships require even more!

After you read this book, I pray you will be able to see red flags quickly and run! It's that simple. In part one of this book, I will share stories about relationships I entertained. At the end of each relationship, I will point out the major red flags and give you advice on how to handle each one! In part two, you will practice pointing out the red flags in a few stories about guys I dated. At the end of this interactive read, I will provide you with a list of questions to ask yourself before you say yes to the date! Don't read this book alone. Find a few of your best friends, and invite them along for the ride!

If you've found yourself in many horrible relationships like me, be encouraged. You deserve the absolute best. Though it may seem tough to walk away, be alone, and wait for the right one, it is so worth it! Well, we have much work to do. Turn the page and let's begin!

PART ONE

RED FLAGS IN RELATIONSHIPS

THE "BABY BOY"

NAME: Demarius

LOCATION: Hempstead, NY

AGE: 29

OCCUPATION: N/A

DEPENDENTS: 2...and one on the way

LENGTH OF RELATIONSHIP: One Year

When Demarius and I first became friends, I wasn't attracted to him at all. He was tall and dark. I thought he looked very interesting, to say the least, but I still gave him a chance. You see, Demarius had that NY swag, and he possessed the gift of gab. That man would run his mouth so much you would think he knew what he talked about. Demarius was very knowledgeable about everything. To top it all off, he knew just what to say to make me feel like a million bucks. Quite naturally, many females were head over heels for Demarius. I can't say that I was *coo coo for Cocoa*

Puffs, but I did take a liking to him. When he asked me out for a date, I agreed.

The First Red Flags

For our first date, we decided to meet in Queens to see a movie. Demarius claimed his car was too old to make it from Long Island to Brooklyn to pick me up, so I would have to ride the train to meet him. The morning before our date, Demarius called me.

"Hey, babe. On your way to the movies, can you get me a long black tee? I want to look nice for you on our first date. It's not much. I think they're only $4.99."

Well, how sweet of him to want to look nice for me on my dime. Cute, right? Wrong. I should have told him to call me back when he was ready to date me the right way, but I didn't. I told him that I would get the shirt for him. At the time, I felt like nothing was wrong with it. After all, it was only $4.99.

I took the train from Brooklyn to Queens with his date shirt in my bag while he drove his very old car from Long Island to the movies. On our first date, we saw an action film. It wasn't my choice, but the

4

date went well. Even though there were warning signs, I decided to ignore them and see what the relationship had in store.

More Red Flags

Demarius claimed time and time again that his car would not make it to Brooklyn, so I always traveled to see him. I didn't have a car at all, but that never stopped me from hopping on a train to see him. He never took a train to see me. I did the absolute most for the relationship very early on. Even though they weren't major things, I soon learned that my bending in the small things made him comfortable with asking me for bigger things.

The more Demarius got comfortable, the more things got interesting. He began to pull several disappearing acts. I wouldn't hear from him for days at a time. Each time, I would be furious. Whenever he decided to pop back up, he always had a beautiful story to explain his absence. Make no mistake, I never believed him. I decided to stay even though I felt in my heart that he was lying to me. I later found out why he kept disappearing. Demarius had a girlfriend who was pregnant with his 3rd child. Yep, baby number three. I knew about the other two children, but the third one (and the girlfriend) came as a shock to me. I still stayed.

Towards the end of our relationship, the girlfriend began to harass me. When Demarius fell asleep, she would use his phone to text me or call me nonstop. Whenever I confronted him about her, he would tell me she was only a friend who did his daughters' hair and watched them when he went job hunting. There was no end to the lies Demarius would tell.

One weekend, I had to leave town to sing at a conference in St. Louis. I was excited to get away from the city, and I looked forward to relaxing. After I had arrived at my beautiful hotel, I laid down to relax before I was scheduled to sing. No sooner than I rested my head on the pillow, I received a call from a blocked number. I ignored the first call, but the number kept calling back. Finally, I decided to answer. To my surprise, it was Demarius' pregnant girlfriend.

"Hello," I answered.

"Where's D?" she asked.

"Girl, he's here in St. Louis with me," I smirked.

"Let me speak to him." She demanded.

"No. He's in the bathroom. May I take a message?" I said asked.

"Listen!" She yelled. "You need to tell him that while he's in St. Louis with you, his son is getting ready to be born. He needs to get here!"

"Okay, love," I replied. "I'll relay the message to him."

After I landed, I had called Demarius at the airport. His phone had been turned off, so I knew she really didn't know where Demarius was. I thought it would be funny to pay her back for all her harassment.

I couldn't get off the phone fast enough before I burst out in laughter. Good for her, I thought. After my laugh was over, my feelings were hurt. Demarius lied so many times about the baby but now, I knew that he was expecting a son. I couldn't believe I was in love with a man who would lie about his son, his own flesh and blood. To me, there was nothing lower. I would love to tell you that I went home, met Demarius, gave him a piece of my mind, and left his dusty butt at the corner, but I didn't. I stayed.

One day, he finally sat me down and told me the truth about his son. "It was a mistake, baby. I'm sorry," he apologized. "One night, me and a friend got drunk. We had a one night stand, and now we are having a baby. There's nothing more to it."

I looked at him in disbelief. I couldn't believe the extent in which that man could lie. I knew the password to his phone and often checked his voicemails. The mother of his son always left love notes for him. So, I knew that they were more than friends. I knew that there was more to it. Demarius loved that girl, and I knew it.

Instead of leaving him, I pushed him to get a job so he could take care of his kids. His resume was crappy, so I helped him fix it up. I even gave him some interview tips. One day, I met up with his mother to give her Demarius' resume. She and I worked near each other. When I handed her the resume, she looked at it, then shook her head in disbelief. "You are too good for him," she said sadly. "Please stop helping him. He is no good, Ashley. He has too many women running around, and too many babies that he cannot afford."

Why on earth would his mother say that? I thought. She was his mother, so she knew him better than I did. However, I still refused to heed her warning. As time went on, I wish I did.

I Finally Ran

A few weeks later, Demarius called me asking for money. This wasn't out of the usual. He had created a habit of asking me for things ever since I bought that black tee for our first date.

"Ashley, I need some help. I'm low on cash, and my girls are in here fighting over the last bagel," he said.

"I thought you were working, D. Where's your money?" I asked.

"I lost the job. I didn't want to tell you because you worked so hard to help me get that job. I'm sorry," he replied.

"What about your mother? Have you called and asked her for help?" I asked. I was determined not to give him money this time.

"My mama is out of town in Canada. Will you please help me this one last time?" He asked.

"I'll call you when I get off work. I'll meet you later with the money or something." I snapped.

In the five years I've worked for my company, not once did his mother and I unintentionally run into each other. Well on this day, I decided to leave work early to meet him with some money. Would you believe who I ran into? Yep, you guessed it – his mother. Some way, we landed on the same train. I hadn't seen her in a while, and she was under the impression that Demarius and I were no longer seeing each other (which is what Demarius told her).

"Oh, I'm just so glad that you decided to leave Demarius alone. My grandson is due any day now. I'm excited to have a new grandbaby, but I am so disappointed in Demarius for making another baby. He can't even take care of the two little girls he already has."

I smiled and didn't say much the entire trip. I was fuming on the inside. I could not wait to get off the train, call Demarius, and finally give him a piece of my mind.

"Hey, D," I said when he answered the phone.

"Ashley, where are you?" he replied.

"How long did you say your mom would be in Canada?" I asked.

"What? Ashley? Are you serious right now? I really need some cash." He said frustrated.

"How long did you say your mom would be in Canada?" I asked again.

"A month, Ashley. She'll be gone for a month. Look, I really need you. The girls need you. Where are you?" he shouted. Needless to say, he was very upset with my slowness in getting my money to him.

I laughed hysterically. "Guess who I was just on the train with, Demarius," I chuckled. "YO MAMA."

I didn't even give him the chance to respond. I blessed him with some good words, hung up the phone, and never spoke to him again.

RED FLAGS RUN

One of the major issues in this relationship was a lack of maturity. Demarius was accustomed to people taking care of him, and because I didn't see the warning signs ahead of time, I fell right into his care rotation. Hindsight is always 20/20. Demarius showed early on that he would expect me to take care of him.

The thing about men like this is that you will never be able to do enough to satisfy them. The moment you turn them down, they will make you feel bad about who you are, and who you have been to them. If we aren't careful, their immaturity can cause us to question our value and worth as a woman.

Many of us encounter these "baby boys" often and don't see it. We see the red flags and just think that it's cute. We find ourselves gloating about how we have to help them, and how they can't seem to survive without us. Make no mistake, this is far from cute. As women, it's easy for us to get caught up in this because we are natural nurturers. If we aren't careful, we can find ourselves smitten with men who want us to care for them just as their mothers did. While this may be fun in the beginning, it will eventually becoming tiring. The man God has for you will not expect you to take care of him. That was never God's design for marriage in the first place. Yes, God designed the woman to help, but the man must have something for her to help him with.

If you are dating with the intention of getting married, keep in mind that maturity will not come when you say *I Do*. Be attentive and watch the signs early. If you see the least bit of immaturity, pray and ask God for clarity and direction. Additionally, don't think that there is anything you can do to force him to grow up. Maturity is a personal journey. It can't be encouraged, or pushed upon anyone. They simply must accept it.

THE DERANGED MAN

NAME: Anthony aka Stacks

LOCATION: Brooklyn, NY

AGE: 36

OCCUPATION: Tire Shop

DEPENDENTS: 1, 2, or 4

LENGTH OF RELATIONSHIP: Five Months

Oh, Anthony. How I met him is irrelevant. Just know that this was by far one of the craziest relationships I've ever had. In just five months, I dealt with more with this man than most women deal with in a ten-year marriage. Anthony was very interesting, to say the least. I should have ran when I noticed how his eyes were weird and bulging. Nevertheless, I gave Anthony a chance.

On our first date, we had dinner at a park in downtown Brooklyn. We went to a Chinese restaurant to pick up a $3.00 container of steamed shrimp and $1.00 Arizona tea. Maybe this is just an appetizer for our meal or something, I thought. Once we got to the park and got settled, and I asked him what we were having. His response? The shrimp and the tea. In his opinion, it was more romantic for us to share.

We were under a bridge having dinner, so I guess he thought the mood was right to profess his love for me. He looked at me with his eyes wide and told me how much he was in love with me and how much he adored me.

This was our first date, and I wasn't there at all. I didn't know what to say, so I just said, "Ummm. Okay. Thank you." I couldn't help but think how weird he was, but I decided to give it a chance and see where it would go. We talked until it got late. As we were walking back to the car, he stopped to use the restroom. Meanwhile, there were two men who looked like they were fresh out of jail doing community service. They tried to talk to me, but before I could get a word out of my mouth, Anthony stormed outside like the Incredible Hulk. He cursed those men out and was ready to fight.

I was highly disgusted with his behavior. Our car ride home was silent. I couldn't help but think about how he had placed me in danger's way. Those men could have had a gun or something.

The very next day (day one after our first date), Anthony bombarded me with phone calls. My silence in the car hinted that I was a bit concerned about his behavior, so he wanted to apologize for his actions. He explained that he was extremely excited about the great new life we would have, and how I would eventually become his wife. I didn't know what to say, so I changed the subject.

Later that day, I was at a friend's house, and he asked to meet me. I was shocked because he didn't have a car. Minutes later, he pulled up in a black Nissan Frontier. He was so excited to drive me around in his new truck. He told me it was paid for and all his.

Day two after our first date, he called me and asked me to pick him up. "What happened to your truck?" I asked.

"Oh, I put it up for a while to save some money." He responded.

By now, I'm thinking either I'm crazy, or something is wrong with this man. Why would someone want to save money on a car that was paid for? I added that to my list of suspicions about him and went to pick him up. When we arrived at his mother's house, he asked me to come upstairs. To my surprise, they were having a mini family reunion, and everyone had already heard about me. Yes, after two days of dating I was meeting the whole family.

Everyone was very nice. They all wanted to know when we were getting married. I just smiled and nodded my head. I wasn't sure what he had told his family, but there was no way I was talking marriage after two days of dating a man. I wasn't that crazy. Things with Anthony went from crazy to even crazier. If he was treating me, we ate McDonald's or Wendy's in my car or at his job. When the meal was on me, he picked a very nice restaurant. His logic behind it? I was his woman, and I needed to make sure he was fed at all times. Additionally, he told me never to call him Anthony. I was to call him Stacks and Stacks only.

After the first two weeks, he had this bright idea of us moving in together. He wanted us to get a room and split the weekly cost. Not an apartment, but a room. "I already have a house, Stacks. There's no need for me to move into a rented room," I said to quickly shut down his stupid idea.

"I know. I'll be the one staying there most of the time. I'm just ready to move out my mom's house. I'll make sure that there is tissue there whenever you come by," he replied.

"No," I said. Stacks clearly didn't get the message the first time, so I just said it as plainly as I could.

Do you think that's crazy? Just wait. There's more. So, after I shut down the dumb room idea, he asked me to take him to the Infiniti dealership to check out some cars. I just paused and looked at him for a few minutes.

"Why do you want to go a dealership? Don't you already have a car that's paid off?" I asked.

He got very upset with me and said that I was challenging his motives. He said it was just something he wanted to do for himself, and shut down. I was accustomed to him reacting this way by now. He never wanted to explain himself fully, so I just let it go. Besides, I was tired of picking him up anyway. If he wanted to go to a dealership, then I figured I might as well support his efforts and take him.

When I asked if I could still go with him, he got super excited. "Yes! This is great baby. Now, I can let you co-sign for the car, and I won't have to ask my aunt!" Another dumb idea that I had to shut down with a quick, "Heck no." He tried to convince me to do it, but I would not budge.

A few days later, I picked him up from another random location. When he got in the car, he was on the phone with someone from out of town. I overheard him talking about property and crops down South. At this point, I was thinking, what on earth does this man really have going on?

When he got off the phone, he told me he had property in Alabama. He had to send money to Alabama monthly so that people could care for his property.

"That's why I'm always low on money." He explained. "I own so many cows, horses, and land that I have to pay a lot of workers to tend the property. To keep myself on a budget, I walk out of the house with only $5 every day, and I leave my bank card with my mother. That way, I won't do any frivolous spending." I almost laughed out loud, but I kept my face straight as to not upset him.

Everything seemed to be cool between us as the days progressed. Stacks took me to meet more family members, we enjoyed our fast food in the car, and of course, we continued to share a can of iced tea. One day, as I sat in my car waiting for him, I got an email from Stacks' email account. It was from someone claiming to be his fiancé. In the email, she expressed that Stacks was a horrible man. She said he had two kids that he didn't take care of and that they were supposed to get married.

Once I read the email, he got in the car. I didn't say much to him. I guess he looked at his phone and realized why I was so upset. He immediately went on a rampage!

"That's my baby sister's friend! She has always liked me, man! I didn't sign out of my email account when I left my mother's apartment!" He shouted.

I didn't respond to him. I just looked at him.

"If you want proof, I'll give it to you! Ashley, do you believe me? I'm not engaged to nobody. I don't have any kids! On everything!" he ranted. He noticed I wasn't moved by his words at all. "Man, dang. This is messed up! I'm going to get my sister to beat her up! She is just trying to mess up our relationship."

I just sat in the car in silence. He suggested that we go to visit his grandfather. I was stunned. Stacks had told me before that he hadn't seen his grandfather in years. His grandfather was in hospice on his death bed. We went over to see him, and my heart just melted. I felt bad for his grandfather. While we were there, Stacks told his grandfather that he was going to marry me one day. His grandfather was in such a bad condition that he couldn't speak much. He just silently agreed.

Two weeks later, Stacks went ghost. I didn't hear from him for a whole month. I was so over it, and part of me was happy that he made the decision for me. Right when I had gotten used to not being a part of his crazy world, he reached out to me. He apologized for going ghost and asked me to meet him at the tire shop. He wanted us to start fresh. Like an idiot, I pranced myself right over to his job and fell back into the same trap again.

The opportunity for me to leave him again came sooner than I expected. I was at work, and I decided to give him a call. We were having a regular conversation. He said something dumb, and I replied, "Okay, Anthony."

Now, remember, I was forbidden ever to call him that. The way he yelled at me, you would have thought I called his mother the B word. He told me to have a nice life, lose his number, and never to call him again. When I hung up the phone, I chuckled to myself. I never understood why he preferred to be called Stacks. He was always Broke. So, I saved his number as Broke in my phone and went on with my day. I was just happy to be free.

Low and behold, fifteen minutes later Broke was calling me. I ignored the first few calls. When I finally answered, he was on the other end acting as though nothing had happened. He wanted to know what took me so long to answer the phone. I quickly reminded him of his request from moments ago, and he laughed.

"Girl, stop playing. You know I am in love with you. I got a little mad. Don't do that again. Remember, you cannot call me Anthony, only Stacks." He said. "I am your man. You are supposed to keep me happy."

One evening, Stacks and I went to McDonald's. He went in to get the food and left his phone in the car. My curiosity got the best of me, so I went through his phone. He was in McDonald's for quite some time, so I had a chance to see every message from Kristen, the girl who claimed to be his fiancé. The messages were very inappropriate, to say the least.

About fifteen minutes had gone by, and he ran out of McDonald's looking like a mad man with no food in his hand. He ran in the car and asked me if he had left his phone. When he saw the phone, he looked at me. He knew I had seen the messages. We got into a heated argument, and I told him to get out of my car. That day, I left his dusty butt right in the middle of downtown Brooklyn. He called me a thousand times, begging me to pick him up, but I told him to call his fiancé. I was proud of myself for leaving him, but a few days later, I took him right back in. I allowed him to con me into believing that what I saw was nothing. Unfortunately, that wasn't the last of the questionable text messages. Weeks later, I saw more messages from a girl stating that he had put bruises on her leg. He responded to the young lady by telling her he was sorry, and how much he loved her. Of course, he lied about those as well, and of course, I stayed and believed him.

Over time (not very much time), our routine continued. We were always yelling at each other, and he was always chastising me for doing something he didn't like. He adored me in public but treated me like crap behind closed doors. I was miserable. Whenever I thought about him, I wanted to throw up. I would break up with him and even block his number, but he always found some way to get in touch with me. Things got scary with our relationship. He even had somebody to follow me home so he could find out where I lived. No matter what he did, I always found myself right back with him again.

Around Valentine's Day, I was completely done with him. No, I hadn't told him yet, but my mind was pretty made up. Holidays and birthdays were weird with this guy. For my birthday, he told me my gift was at his mother's house for about a week, and I never got it. For Christmas, he told me he didn't celebrate it. The days leading to Valentine's Day, he constantly reminded me that he didn't celebrate that either, so I didn't need to expect anything from him. On Valentine's Day, we hung out at his tire shop. Weirdly enough, throughout the day, I constantly heard him wishing every woman a Happy Valentine's Day. I shook my head at that broke man and kept it pushing.

I slowly began to drift away. I stopped calling and coming to the shop. He didn't seem to notice or try to reach back out until the day of his birthday. He called me to take him shopping and to pick up his gifts from everyone. As much as I didn't want to, I drove him around Brooklyn. I took him where he wanted to go, and even helped him pay for a coat he wanted. I must give him a little credit though. He did buy us a small frozen yogurt to share. I hated every minute of his birthday rendezvous, and I could not wait to drop him off.

After his birthday, I stopped calling him completely. We only talked when he called. He would ask to see me, and I would make up some lie about work. Finally, one day I texted him: I guess it's safe to say we are no longer together. Even though my actions had already said that we were over, actually hearing me say it sent him through the roof. That crazy switch in his head clicked completely on. He called me nonstop. Seeing his name pop up on my screen made my stomach hurt. He would make threats on my voicemail, cry, beg me to come back, and request me to be a woman about our break-up. The voicemails were endless.

I was terrified of him. He harassed me for months. He stalked me, watched me leave my house, followed me around, and everything. I was so worried that I cried all the time. I didn't tell my family what was going on because I didn't want them to know what I had gotten myself into. Finally, I changed my phone number, and the harassing calls stopped.

Almost a year and a half had gone by, and I was finally free of Stacks, or so I thought. One morning, I went to run errands and found a parking ticket envelope on my car window. I thought that was strange. When I opened it, and saw who the letter was from, my heart dropped. It was Stacks, giving me his new number and requesting me to call him. This totally freaked me out. I never called him, but I constantly looked over my shoulder. Things got so bad that I didn't even want to go home.

A few months later, I was in the parking lot at Target, and I heard someone calling me.

"Excuse me miss. Do you need some help?" As soon as I turned and realized who it was, I began to pray. It was Stacks.

"Ashley! You didn't follow my instructions. You are supposed to be my woman! Ashley! Ashley! I know you hear me!" he yelled.

I ignored him and rushed to my car which was parked by the police station. Luckily for me, it was the holidays, and the police department had set up stations at bigger stores for shopper safety. As I rushed to my car, I still heard him calling me from a distance.

"Ashley! Ashley! I know you hear me!" Stacks shouted.

I made it to my car in record time and sped off. My heart was beating a mile a minute. After two years, that man still acted as though we were still together. It was clearer than ever to me that Stacks was mentally ill and needed some help. Needless to say, I've never heard from him since, and I am glad about it.

RED FLAGS RUN

There's nothing cute or special about a crazy, obsessive, and temperamental man. With Anthony, I saw early on that he had anger issues, but I chose to ignore them. This situation could have quickly been deadly. Believe it or not, there are many Anthony's out there, and there are many Ashley's out there willing to give them a chance. Ladies, don't be one of those Ashley's.

Many women accept obsessive behavior because they feel as though it validates the man's love for them. This is not the case. Men who show signs of being obsessive and jealous are usually this way for a reason. Nine times out of ten, it's because they are hiding secrets of their own. Anthony did many things to let me know he had obsessive behavior. The way he chastised me, how he constantly wanted me to cater to him, and not to mention the way he blew up on those guys on our first date. Ladies, you don't want to get involved with a man with a bad temper. If his anger is that easily triggered, what makes you think he won't get that angry with you someday?

30

One of the best analogies I can think of is the lady who kept a gorilla as a pet. A while back, her story was all over the news. One day, the lady came home and the gorilla literally ripped her face off. Everyone felt some type of way about the gorilla, but no one seemed to remember that the gorilla was a wild animal, and that eventually, his wild nature would overcome all the woman's efforts to treat him like a domestic household pet.

The same is with an aggressive and obsessive man. It doesn't matter how sweet he is to you, if you see the red flags, run! The best way you can help him is to guide him to the nearest professional. Don't put yourself in harm's way trying to be a hero and love a man to wholeness. This type of stuff requires true deliverance from God and maybe even some serious psychological counseling.

THE PLAYBOY

NAME: Byron

LOCATION: Atlanta, Ga

AGE: 27

OCCUPATION: Dog Breeder/Ex Pro-Football Player

DEPENDENTS: none

LENGTH OF RELATIONSHIP: Five Months

Being 4'11, I had a thing for taller guys. Well, Byron fit the bill. He was 6'3, and light skinned with freckles. He was cute. Physically, the only thing I didn't like was his hair. He wore this weird hair style, so I preferred him wearing a fitted cap. Byron was very charming. The man spoke with authority, and I loved it.

We met via Facebook through mutual friends. I know it sounds weird, but I knew many people who met on Facebook, became close friends, fell in love, and got married. So, I decided to give computer love a chance. Via Facebook, Byron took an interest in me, and I was flattered. We exchanged numbers, and it was on from there. We spoke every day. What was so unique about him as a man was that he was a talker. He loved to chat for hours on end.

Red Flags

During our Skype chats, I learned that he was a dog breeder. I always saw him at home taking care of his dogs. He had gotten hurt playing pro-football, so he bred pit bulls to make extra cash until he healed. Byron assured me he was financially stable, and that he made thousands in his business. I didn't know much about dog breeding, so I just assumed he was being honest.

He lived with his parents, but he planned to move back to Germany once he got the okay from his physical therapist. I asked him for his professional football pictures, but he always had an excuse as to why he couldn't find or share them with me. I eventually stopped asking about the pictures. One thing we often talked about was his ex-fiance, Laura. Apparently, she had cheated on him, so he broke off the engagement. He said he tried to take her back, but she wasn't willing to work out their issues. I often wondered if he was over her, but he assured me that he was. However, he would often compare us, or bring up things that she would do. The more we chatted, the more I grew suspicious of Byron, but that didn't stop me from picking up the phone when he called.

More Red Flags

Two and a half months after we met via Facebook, we planned to meet in person! I was super excited. With us being so far apart, it was hard to see each other. I was scheduled to sing at a conference in Atlanta, GA, but honestly, I was more excited about spending real time with Byron than attending and singing.

When I arrived in Atlanta, we spoke throughout the entire day. We were so anxious to see each other. As I was getting ready for him to come pick me up for our first date, I got a text from him saying that he had lost his wallet at McDonald's. I felt my heart drop. "Well, don't come, Byron," I told him. "I don't want you driving without your Driver's License."

"No baby, I always leave my driver's license and social security card in the car. So, I only lost my cards and money," he responded. I encouraged him just to come and hang out. We didn't have to spend money. I just wanted to see him. He insisted on taking me to dinner and told me that he would ask his parents for money.

I was staying at my sister's house during the conference, but I didn't communicate with her to explain where I was going or who I was going with. After singing, the girls and I walked to a restaurant close to the hotel where the conference took place. I told everyone I was not eating because I would be eating dinner with my friend later. When I got the text that he was close, I jetted and went outside to meet him. I never said goodbye to my sister or any of the girls. I just took off. I was that excited!

A few minutes later, he pulled up in an old car that made noise. I heard him coming before I saw him pulling up. Before we met, he had told me about all his luxury cars, so I was a bit confused. Oh well, I thought. I was just excited about seeing him.

He got out to hug me, and it felt like we hugged for about two minutes. He squeezed me tight, and I was immediately lost in the smell of his cologne. I loved a man who smelled good. As I got into the car, I thought to myself, "This is it! I really like my new boo/future husband!"

We drove around downtown Atlanta trying to decide where we would eat. He showed me around a bit, and we finally decided to sit and eat at a southern soul food spot. When we pulled up to the restaurant, I noticed a small wallet under the dashboard, but I said nothing. I just took a mental note. He took my hand, gazed into my eyes, and said, "Baby, I didn't get the money from my parents. Can you take care of the bill tonight?"

Like a dummy, I agreed. Throughout the night, he constantly told me how beautiful I was. We had great conversation, and everything was beautiful until it came time to pay the bill. I dreaded having to pay for our meal. It just didn't feel right. I whipped out my debit card and handed it to the waiter before he barely sat the bill on the table. I just wanted to get it over with. I shook the idea of him playing me out of my head and was determined to enjoy the rest of the night.

After dinner, he apologized for not being able to pay. He promised to make it up to me once he got new debit cards. Then, he proceeded to go down a list of things he had to do for the weekend which required him to have money. He asked if he could borrow at least $150.

I just stared at him in disbelief. Just like that, this man had gotten a meal out of meal and was requesting me to take care of his weekend too. I sighed out of frustration.

"If you can't, I totally understand." He said. "As your man, I would do anything I can for you. I hope that you would do the same for me. It would only be this one time. Baby, you know I'm good for it."

"Okay," I said. "I'll give you what I have." I reached into my purse and handed him the $100 the church had given us for meals. He leaned over to kiss me, and just like that, I forgot about all my frustration. His kiss was so nice that I think I actually floated.

By this point, it was getting late. My phone died, and I was certain my sister was worried and looking for me. She didn't know where I was or who I was with. He dropped me off at my sister's house. Of course, my sister fussed after I told her where I was. She was worried, and she didn't know what to tell my dad when he called to check on us. I apologized and went to bed. Many emotions ran through my mind. I was annoyed with myself for paying for dinner and giving him the money. I was excited about seeing him again. I felt all warm and fuzzy inside, but I still couldn't shake feeling like I was getting played.

I was in Atlanta for four days. In that time, I only saw Byron twice. He was so busy that he couldn't hang out. On my last day, he picked me up, and we went to a lounge. My sister, aunt, and a friend decided to meet us there. They were itching to meet him. I'm glad they pulled up after I paid the bill (again). He made a first great impression on them. They almost swooned when he asked for the honor of getting me to the airport safely.

Little did they know, he had asked me for more money and wanted to make sure he got it before I left. Right when I thought he had forgotten about the money, he leaned over and asked, "Hey, are you still going to be able to give me the money?"

I handed him some money, and he gave me a kiss. This time, it didn't make me float. I was starting to feel used. I spent majority of the plane ride home trying to convince myself that Byron and I had something special. I couldn't understand why he felt so comfortable asking me for money our first time meeting. Don't get me wrong. I was glad he wasn't prideful. However, something about the whole situation just didn't sit right with me.

As we continued our long-distance relationship, the money requests grew. He even requested me to Western Union money, and I did. I never disclosed any of this information with my sister, my aunt, or any of my friends in fear of them confirming what I already knew.

During this time, my sister was transitioning into a new season of her life, so I decided to go to visit her in Atlanta again. When I told Byron the news, he was ecstatic. He began to make amazing plans for us. His calls increased, and he just couldn't stop telling me how excited he was to see me again.

I Finally Let Go

The day before I left, Byron texted me asking me to call him. I figured it must be pretty serious because he knew I was at work. When I called him, he explained that he was being hit with a large fine and had to pay the court system $1,000.

"Oh wow," I said. "That's messed up. How are you going to pay it?"

"Baby, I don't have it." He explained. "Would you be able to pay it?"

By this point, I was annoyed. "Where the heck do you think I'm going to get that kind of money. I don't have it, Byron."

"Come on, Ashley. Please, I need this. If you want, let's draft a contract. I'm going to pay you back. If not, you can take me to court. I need this," he pleaded.

"What about the engagement ring from your ex? Can't you pawn that?" I asked.

"I thought about that, but I already gave it to my mother as a gift," he replied.

That's interesting, I thought to myself. Why on earth would he give his married mother an

41

engagement ring? Additionally, he had told me previously that he kept the ring in a safe. "Well take it back," I suggested.

This ticked him off. He couldn't believe that I would suggest taking the ring back from his mother. I was thinking with my heart and not my head, so I agreed to draft the contract once I got to Georgia.

When I arrived, I texted him, and he came over to my sister's house to see me. This trip was no different than the last trip. I filled up his little "hoopty" with gas, we ate fast food on my dime, and I paid for every activity he came up with for us. My sister even let me use her Lexus to see him, in which he took and left me at my sister's house while he drove around handling business. We hung out with my family a lot, but I never even met his mother. We even went to his house a few times, but I sat in the car as he went inside. One time, he did bring out two of his dogs so that we could walk them.

So finally, the day arrived for him to go to court. "Well, let me get dressed so we can go together," I told him. His eyes got big, and he jumped up saying he had to take care of something. Hours rolled by, I did not hear from Byron. I got frustrated, called my aunt, and told her about everything. She was livid! I finally accepted the truth of my situation and decided to wait for Byron to call me back. He finally called to ask me if he could come pick up the money. Instead of giving him the money, I told him just to give me the name of the court and I would pay the fee online. He immediately got belligerent with me, and we started to argue. I realized that he didn't have court, he just wanted to use me for money. We argued, and he called me all types of names. I never heard from him or saw him during that visit.

Just like that, he was done with me. No more going to Germany. No more wedding planning. Byron was using me from day one. I was so hurt that weekend, that I ended up getting a tattoo before I left Atlanta, Georgia. It took a while to get over it, but I was just glad that I wised up before doing something I would regret. I eventually forgave him for my own peace of mind, but I had no desire of reconnecting with him.

Years later, I saw him post something on Facebook. It was his engagement pictures with none other than Laura, his ex-fiancé. I thought I would be devastated,

but I wasn't. I was happy for them…just scared for
her pockets!

RED FLAGS RUN

From the jump, Byron was obviously still attached to his ex. Here's the thing ladies, we are all guilty of having rebounds. We get out of relationships, and instead of healing properly, we jump into another relationship. It's kind of our way of ridding ourselves of the pain and disappointment from the last relationship. As you read through the rest of the stories, you will probably pick up that I was guilty of this type of serial dating. Here's the thing, men are too.

We must be aware of men that are still grieving from a previous relationship. Studies show that men grieve relationship much longer after women do. In all actuality, once the man actually starts to grieve, the woman is probably already healed and over the situation.

In my situation, Byron was still not over his ex. The red flags were evident when he constantly talked about her. That should have been my first sign to run.

I thank God that Byron and I weren't together that long. Even though our break-up hurt, I wasn't attached enough to be devastated about his reconnection with his ex.

Ladies, if a man shows any sign that he may still be interested in his ex, back off. You don't have to compete or measure up to anyone. Even though he may not compare you on purpose, it's hard for him not to do so if his ex is still on his mind. Kindly let him know that you are not interested in dating, at the time, but you would be happy to give it a try once he got over his ex. Be honest and save yourself a lot of heartache in the long run.

THE LIAR

NAME: Ja'Kel aka Ja'Kir aka Ja'Liar
LOCATION: New York, NY
AGE: 30
OCCUPATION: Computer Programmer
DEPENDENTS: 1
LENGTH OF RELATIONSHIP: 1 year, 2 months

One night, I went out with a few of my girls to an event in the city to celebrate our friend's 30th birthday. We were having a great time when this handsome brother walked up to me and introduced himself as Ja'Kel. He just so happened to be celebrating his 30th birthday too. When I first saw Ja'Kel, he was pleasant to my eyes. He was dressed nice, very sweet, and charming. That night, we exchanged numbers. The very next day, he texted me to let me know that he enjoyed meeting me, and wanted to stay in touch. From that point on, we talked on the phone and sent text messages to each other non-stop.

RED FLAGS

After about two weeks, he told me he was heading to visit his mom and wanted to see me. She lived in the projects close to my house so we decided to meet up there. Once I arrived at his mother's building, he came downstairs. We sat in the car and talked for hours. He was very talkative. It's like he wanted to tell me everything about himself. He was just so upfront. He told me about his daughter, his biracial ethnicity, his time in jail, his allergies, his family, and everything. Among the many things he shared, he also told me that he was afraid of being hurt. He hadn't been in a relationship for two years because he wanted to wait for the right one. He said so much that night, but I didn't make any major responses. I just took a mental note of everything. Right off back, something's didn't add up, but I didn't think much of it. I mean hey, the man was pouring out his soul. It's possible he got some stuff mixed up.

In my head, this man had it all together. Even though he was a little off in some places, he was better than most men. He was well dressed, had a great job, loved his mother, and best of all, he took care of his daughter. His job paid for him to go to school part-time to advance in his field, and eventually advance his pay at the company. I really liked him, but I told him that I wanted to take things slow because I'd just gotten out of a rocky relationship. He respected my desires. That night, I left Ja'Kel and felt quite optimistic about our future together. Thoughts of us together consumed my mind. He was all I could think about.

For the next few months, we spent every day together. It was summertime, so I was shocked. Most men preferred to be outside and available, but that was not the story with Ja'Kel. He took me to meet his friends, family, his grandmother, his beloved daughter, and even his daughter's mother.

One day, I met his mother in the Bronx. "Hello! I'm Ja'Kir's mother. We met a while ago! How are things with you and my son?" she greeted me.

I stopped for a second. Did she say Ja'Kir? I just shook it off as her accent and thought nothing else of it. As time went on, I began to spend more and more time with his family, particularly, his Aunt MiMi.

49

The more I listened, the more I noticed that she also referred to him as Ja'Kir. She also said things about Ja'Kel that made me raise my eyebrows. Again, I didn't say much, I only listened.

Though I didn't mind spending time with his family, sometimes, he would take my car and leave me there alone with them for two to three hours at a time. I would call his phone or text him, and he would not answer. His aunt was cool, but she was crazy, and she smoked all day long. I would get so aggravated with him, but by the time he got back he would have a nice surprise for me, and I would forget how angry I was.

More Red Flags

Ja'Kel had his issues, but the man had so many areas that made up for them. He would text me every morning at five a.m. when he woke up, and he would text me all day long. He never called during work hours, and I respected that. After all, he worked on Wall Street. I'd worked on Wall Street for about seven years myself, so I understood. One day, I asked him about the company he worked for, but he said the name so fast, that the company didn't sound familiar to me. I never brought it up again.

When we first met, he told me about the trip he planned to go to the Dominican Republic with his brother and close friend. A few weeks before he was scheduled to go on his trip, he sent me a very disturbing text. His younger brother, Damien (the one who lived with him) got arrested for killing one of two guys who came to fight him at Ja'Kel's apartment. He then proceeded to tell me he was going to do everything in his power to get his brother out of jail. Now, Ja'Kel explained to me before his brother's arrest that he had a large amount of money put away, 200k to be exact. So, I knew he had the money to get his brother out.

A few days later, Ja'Kel texted me and told me that he had three days to get all his stuff out of his apartment and move. I offered to help him move, but he refused my help aggressively. He told me that he would put his stuff in storage and stay with his other aunt for a few days. I was a bit disappointed because I would never get to see the lavish apartment he had bragged about. After he moved, he seemed so depressed and faced with hard decisions. I encouraged him, I was there for him, and I vowed not to make any added issues for him. I tried to stay out of his way. I sent him encouraging text messages every chance I got. It sucked that I had to be strong for him, but I loved the man. I knew I was woman enough to handle the challenge and see him through his rough season. Ja'Kel's life continued to spiral downhill. He stopped going to school and called out of work. He took a month vacation. He told me his boss was cool with him and gave him time off because of his situation. I know being at a job for eight years is great, but I never heard of being out of work for a month to hang out just because your boss is cool.

Things only got worse for him. He said Damien's bail was set at 225k and he had to take the money out of his savings to save his younger brother. He felt so passionately about his younger brother because he said he had taken care of him since birth. I have a younger brother whom I love dearly, but I didn't understand why he would empty his savings to help someone who had killed another man.

"Babe, just make sure that you won't regret this decision," I advised him.

"He's my baby brother, Ashley! I would do anything for him. I am my brother's keeper. I've just got to get him out of there." Ja'Kel replied.

"Okay, I understand," I said sympathetically. "It's your money. So, it's your decision."

After scrambling to get the rest of the money from other relatives, he got his brother out of jail, moved in with his aunt, and spoke nothing of his brother whom he didn't even see anymore. Now and then, I would ask about his brother. He had a lame excuse for everything in regards to Damien. He claimed he didn't have details about the trial or anything else. I don't know about you, but if I invested 225k into someone, they would be taped to my car door. However, that was not the case with Ja'Kel. He seemed to just be happy that his brother was free.

Of course, 225k is a lot of money, so Ja'Kel explained to me that he had to start from scratch. He even asked me if I was concerned about being with him now that he was broke. I assured him that it wasn't an issue for me and that I didn't care about the money. I honestly didn't. Ja'Kel was always doing nice things for me. He even gave me money every week, just because. I never asked for it. Even after he bailed his brother out of jail, he still gave me money. He was different from most of the guys I dated, so I made up in my mind to be there for the long haul.

One day, Ja'Kel asked me to pick him up from his new residence with his aunt. I was excited that I would finally get to see his new place. When I arrived, he told me to stay in the car. He didn't want me to meet this aunt or come upstairs. Well, of course, I was upset. He noticed my disappointment when he got in the car, and explained that the house was very junky. He said he was embarrassed for me to see the condition in which he now lived. I was very confused. He had taken me to every relative's house in Brooklyn. These relatives lived in the projects. All of their apartments were old, junky, and filthy. As a matter of fact, his mother's apartment was the worse of them all. I went one time and met every creepy crawler Brooklyn had to offer. Now, he was in a place that looked ten times better from the outside alone, and he was embarrassed for me to come inside? This was definitely a red flag for me.

One Sunday evening after church, I went to the Bronx with him to visit his Aunt MiMi. As usual, he sat down for about five minutes, then jetted out of the door and left me with his Aunt MiMi. I sat in the living room with her, listened to her chatter, and watched her go through about five cigarettes in one setting. After about four hours, I started to get upset. She could tell that I was livid, so she got upset too.

"You need to ask Ja'Kir where he is taking your car every time you two come to visit!" she said. "Does he even have a license yet?

By this point, I'd had enough. It was clear that she was saying Ja'Kir and not Ja'Kel.

"Wait. Why do you all keep calling him Ja'Kir?" I asked.

"Well that's his name, baby," she explained. "His middle name actually."

I was super shocked. I explained to her the whole "Ja'Kel" story and all she could do was shake her head.

"Listen, the boy's name is Ja'Kir," she told me. "He doesn't like to be called by his first name, but the whole family refers to him as Ja'Kir, his legal middle name. Ja'Kel is not either of his names. I don't know where he got Ja'Kel from."

I was heated! This whole time, I thought his name was Ja'Kel. He said Ja'Kel. He introduced himself as Ja'Kel. My entire family knew him as Ja'Kel. My friends knew him as Ja'Kel.

Aunt MiMi saw that I was shocked. I told her how I met him, and about a few other things Ja'Kel had told me about his life. Afterwards, she proceeded to give me a mouth full.

"Child, I don't know what kind of lies that man has been telling you," Aunt MiMi said. "He doesn't have a license. He works at the 99-cent store. As a matter of fact, that's where he told us he met you. I don't want to get in the middle of your business, but you need to check that."

"I can't believe Ja'Kel, I mean Ja'Kir, whatever his name is..." I began to cry.

His aunt cut me off. "Baby, just call him Ja'Liar. 'Cause that's all he does," she laughed.

She encouraged me to find out the truth. "You've got to check him now, Ashley, before this goes any further."

And check him I did! When he finally got back, I jumped in the car and let him have it! He got angry and frustrated.

"MiMi is lying about everything! She does drugs, so you can't believe what she says," he exclaimed. "My family doesn't know anything about me. I told them I worked at a 99-cent store so they would stop asking me for money. Everything Aunt MiMi told you was a complete lie. She is crazy, and she likes drama. Why would I leave you over there with her if I was hiding so much?"

He actually made sense. I understood about him lying about his finances. I had to fib about my actual funds to keep men from asking me for handouts. I couldn't see him working at a 99-cent store because the man was always taking me shopping, putting money in my hand, and buying me nice things. In our whole relationship, he never asked me for money. I decided to believe him, and I stopped questioning him about the stuff MiMi told me. My biggest concern now was that if MiMi was so crazy, why did he constantly leave me with her. Instead of pressing the issue, I dropped it and decided to be a woman about the whole situation. I had a good man. I wasn't about to let some petty stuff get in the way of our relationship.

Weeks later, we were sitting in the car, and I noticed his driver's license was wedged between the seats, so I reached for it. He realized what I was reaching for and we both began to fight to get the license. We were literally in the car tussling over his driver's license. I finally got the license in my hand, and this man did the unthinkable. He bit me on my hand! I was so shocked that I immediately let it go. I looked at him, and he looked mad crazy. I was infuriated and demanded an explanation.

"I didn't want you to see my ugly picture," he tried to laugh it off.

That story was lame, and I realized then that he was hiding something. I let it go. I knew that I would find out sooner than later. Funny enough, I found out much sooner than I expected. Later that week, Ja'Kel took my cousin and me to Harlem to a lounge. My cousin and Ja'Kel hit it off when they first met. They became good friends. Whenever I came around without him, she always asked where he was and how he was doing. Of course, I covered for him. I never told them what was going on with us. That night, the two of them got ridiculously drunk, and I had to be the designated driver. I put the two of them in the back seat, and they fell asleep. When I got to Ja'Kel's house to drop him off, I noticed his license in his coat pocket. I quickly pulled it out. It wasn't even a license. It was a NY state ID. My heart dropped. In my hand was proof about three things: He wasn't 30, he was 26. He didn't have a license to drive. His name was not Ja'Kel. I was so hurt. I didn't want to make a scene in front of my cousin, so I shoved the license back into his wallet and got him up so that he could go home.

Later the next day, I confronted him about my findings. He confessed about the name part. His name was Ja'Kir. As for everything else, he claimed his friend at the DMV changed his information so that he could work for the company where he was currently employed. I calmed down. Once again, I let it go. I was in love, and I believed in my heart that we could work through it.

Despite my desire to work through it, Ja'Kir was not interested in talking things out. Whenever I brought up the things he lied about, he would get upset, shut down, and not speak to me for days at a time. I googled his zodiac sign and realized that as an Aries, this was typical behavior. I don't believe in zodiac signs, but your girl was desperate for some type of explanation! So I dismissed his actions and decided to keep trying with him.

When I didn't hear from him, I got so worried. I would call his Aunt MiMi to see if she had heard from him or seen his daughter. Every time I called, she told me how much she loved me and wished that I would walk away from her nephew. She told me over and over again how I was the best thing that had ever happened to her nephew, but he was no good for me. She encouraged me to leave him and start fresh, but I did not listen to her. I was too involved with him. I loved him. I accepted his lies. Ja'Kir professed his love for me whenever we talked. I would daydream about the day he made me his wife.

He would always tell me how he wanted to work hard to provide a great life for me and his daughter, Jada. Knowing his daughter also made it hard for me to walk away from him. The first time I met her, she looked at her daddy and said, "Are you going to marry, Ashley? I like her, daddy." At the root of it all, I had given Ja'Kir so much of me and my time. I didn't want to start over. I was confident that I could help him fix whatever mess and lies he had gotten himself into.

As my 30th birthday approached, I was ecstatic! This was the first birthday that I had dating a man who was financially stable. Even though I could afford anything I wanted, I was excited to see what Ja'Kir would get me. I'd never had a man actually do anything for me for my birthday (other than family, of course). I knew that this birthday would be something special.

I had planned to spend the weekend before my birthday with my sisters and friends in Atlanta, and spend the day of my birthday with Ja'Kir. Before I left for Atlanta, Ja'Kir asked me if I wanted my present before I left. I wanted to wait until my actual birthday, so I told him I would get it when I got back.

The first night I arrived in Atlanta, I didn't hear a word from Ja'Kir which was unusual. I called him the next day, and he didn't respond. I texted him, and he did not reply. I shook it off as maybe he was busy and went on with my day. I was having so much fun that I really didn't notice it. Saturday morning, my sister planned a spa day for myself and a few other girls, so I turned my phone off and put it in the locker. When we left the spa, I turned on my phone and saw a crazy text from Ja'Kir.

"Baby, I'm sorry I didn't respond. My little brother, Damien, got killed yesterday. It's been crazy. I'm sorry I am just now hitting you up." I immediately panicked. I called his phone numerous times and got no response. I told my sister what happened, and she was just as shocked as I was. I sent him a text expressing that I was cutting my trip short and heading to be with him. He immediately responded telling me there was nothing I could do. He wanted me to enjoy my trip and said we would talk when I got back. I was shocked, and I had a weird feeling that everything was not as it seemed.

My trip was finally over, and I was so ready to get back to NY to check on my man. I called him to let him know I was on the way. When he didn't answer, I got so worried. I knew how much he loved his little brother, and I prayed that he hadn't done anything crazy. I called Aunt MiMi to check on Ja'Kir and the family. I could only imagine what they were going through.

"Hello," Aunt MiMi answered the phone.

"Hey, Aunt MiMi. This is Ashley. How are you guys holding up? Is there anything I can do?" I asked sadly.

"Do for what, baby? We are fine. Are you okay?" she asked confused.

"Well, Ja'Kir told me about what happened to Damien. I was just calling to make sure you guys were okay." I replied. Now, I was starting to get confused. This woman didn't sound like she had just lost a nephew.

"Damien? Who is Damien? What happened to Damien?" she replied.

"Damien. Your nephew? Ja'Kir's brother? He got killed two days ago?" I said. I was cautious not to say too much. I didn't know if they had told her yet. It was two days after the murder, so I figured the whole family knew by now.

"I don't know anything about that. Let me call around and see what's going on," Aunt MiMi replied.

Ten minutes later, she called me back.

"Ashley, I have never heard of Ja'Kir having a brother named Damien. We only know one Damien. He lives down the block. He is alive and well and still giving people hell. I don't know who Ja'Kir is talking about." Aunt MiMI explained.

I got off the phone with her and boarded my plane. I felt like I was stuck between a rock and a hard place. I wanted to comfort Ja'Kir, but I felt like it was all a lie. I felt it strongly, but how could I tell the man he was lying. It was such a sensitive issue. I thought back to how Ja'Kir went out of his way to get Damien out of jail. I thought about how passionate he was about caring for his brother. There was no way I could even bring myself to asking him if he was lying.

On the other hand, if he was so close to this brother, how come none of his family knew anything about him? It just wasn't adding up. I thought myself into a headache. I was in the air, so there was nothing I could do about it then. I took a nap and relaxed for the rest of my flight.

When I got back to Brooklyn, I went as fast as I could to get to Ja'Kir. When I saw him, I threw my arms around him and held him. To my surprise, he acted as though nothing had happened. I thought it was maybe a part of his grieving process, so I didn't bring it up. After days had gone by, I brought it up, but he was very short with me. From then on, he didn't bring it up unless I did. He left for awhile to go to New Jersey to find out who killed his brother. He also told me that he was busy getting the money together for his brother's funeral.

A week or so had gone by, and there was still no talk of a funeral for Damien. I knew about a situation that took place maybe a month before where a young lady's kid's father was murdered in Queens, NY after a party. Crime Stoppers paid for the funeral in its entirety. I simply suggested to Ja'Kir that I would call them to see if they could help fund Damien's funeral, being that he was murdered. Ja'Kir straight panicked. He shouted that he didn't want to do that and that he would take care of everything. I explained to him that if he took any longer, the city would dump Damien's body and there would be no honoring his life.

Two weeks after my birthday, Ja'Kir called me in panic when he finally returned to his aunt's apartment. He was literally in tears. He told me he tore the house up looking for the gift he had purchased me. It had mysteriously disappeared. I had heard that lie so many times, and I couldn't hide my disappointment. I told him that I didn't believe him, and that he could save his lie for someone else. He told me off and hung up the phone. Moments later, he sent me a picture of a beautiful ring in a box on his dresser. Though the ring was stunning, I couldn't get over what I saw on the dresser. I noticed the box of cologne I purchased for him and some feminine products as well. I got so upset, but I never said a word. I couldn't help but think that the ring was actually for the woman who owned the feminine products on the dresser. I realized that he was still heartbroken due to losing a brother that no one had heard of, so I again decided to be a woman about it. It just wasn't the time to press the issue, so I took a mental note and let it go.

Needless to say, I never got my gift and had started to wish I had gotten it before I left for Atlanta. I felt horrible for even thinking that, but something just didn't seem right to me. I shook off my feelings and continued to be the caring girlfriend I always was. I told quite a few of my co-workers, family, and friends about what happened to Damien, and they all extended their sympathy to Ja'Kir. They wanted to know when the funeral would be and if there was anything they could do to help. Of course, I had no answers for them, but I told them that I would let them know as soon as I found out anything.

A month went by, and I still hadn't heard anything about a funeral for Damien. When my family asked, I simply lied and said that the funeral had already taken place. I told them that because of the circumstances, it was a private ceremony with just his family present.

Finally, it was Thanksgiving Weekend. I decided to invite Ja'Kir to the house to meet my father. He had already met the rest of the family. They knew him, and they loved him. This was a big deal to me because I was 30 years old and had never invited anyone over for Thanksgiving to meet my family.

When I asked Ja'Kir, he quickly agreed. Deep down inside, I felt like he would make an excuse or go ghost the day of, but to my surprise, he didnt't. For the first time in his life, my father was at a loss for words when I walked in the house with Ja'Kir. He couldn't believe that I was introducing him to a man. He was even more shocked to see how everyone else was talking to Ja'Kir and hugging on him. My dad asked a thousand questions and wondered how everyone else had already met him. We all laughed at my dad and sat down for dinner.

During dinner, Ja'Kir began to talk about the work he did with computers. I winced in my seat and prayed that he wouldn't say anything dumb. My mother worked with computers at Macintosh when I was a baby. If he said something dumb, she would pick up on it. As I listened to him and watched my mother's reactions, I realized that he was not making any sense at all. My mother smiled and looked at me out of the corner of her eye. I immediately changed the subject. God knows I didn't want to create another lie for Ja'Kir. Besides, nothing got past my mother.

After dinner, we had to leave to go to the Bronx and spend time with his daughter. My cousins were a little sad because we always spent the holidays together, but they understood.

As soon as we got to the apartment where everyone would spend Thanksgiving, Ja'Kir told me to go upstairs, and he would be right back. Well, I lost it. "Heck No!" I shouted. "I could have stayed with my family in a clean house! I will not be going upstairs to sit with your family by myself."

He seemed to have understood. We went upstairs, Ja'Kir said hello to everyone, kissed his daughter on the head, and snuck out the house while I was greeting his family. When I noticed he was gone, I was infuriated. I sat in one of the nastiest apartments I had ever seen in my life. It was so gross that I sat in one spot and did not move. There were large roaches crawling along the walls in packs. There was a huge pipe in the middle of what appeared to be a kitchen. They had a massive pit bull tied up to the pipe. Every time someone walked in, the dog would growl and try its best to break free. I wasn't sure what the pipe was connected to, but I prayed the dog wouldn't detach the pipe from the wall. In the midst of all of that, there were dozens of pans of food. I don't even know where they cooked everything because the only thing I saw in the kitchen was a stove, I can't even remember seeing a refrigerator.

I sat with Jada and let her play with my phone. She wanted to download every game she could think of, and I let her. I felt so bad that her daddy had left her on Thanksgiving Day. As the hours passed, I got extremely frustrated. I was fuming as I watched every neighborhood crackhead walk in, say hi, and grab a plate of food. I didn't speak to anyone, and they could tell I was very upset. Finally, Jada's mother walked in. I had only met her one time, but she knew exactly who I was. After she spoke to the family, she turned to me and said, "Hey, aren't you Ja'Kir's girl?"

"Yes. Ashley. We've met. How are you?" I asked.

"I'm fine, girl," she said. "Listen, I don't have anything against you, but Ja'Kir ain't no good. Could you please ask him to spend some time with his daughter? He promises to pick up Jada and never does. He also promises to buy her stuff, but always has an excuse about why he doesn't."

She expressed her concerns, and she and I had a long chat. I was so shocked. Ja'Kir insisted that he was with his daughter every chance he got. I began to recount the many times he left me to go pick her up. Now, his child's mother was saying something totally different. Someone was lying, and my gut told me it was Ja'Kir. I was at my wit's end at this point. My Thanksgiving had gone from good to horrible.

As I sat there thinking about everything Jada's mother had shared, I began to get sleepy. I noticed it was about two a.m., and I had to be at work that morning. I called Ja'Kir until my phone died. He had always left me with his family for a long time, but never this late. I actually began to think something bad had happened to him. His family asked me to call the hospitals and even insinuated that maybe he got arrested for driving without a license.

Jada's mother had left Jada with me, and the little girl had fallen asleep in my lap. The two of us sat there on that nasty couch. Finally, he strolled in, picked his daughter up, kissed her, and told me it was time to go. I looked at him with rage in my eyes. I wanted to fight him and leave his lying behind there. When we got in the car, I went off on him and told him how he disappointed his daughter and me. He apologized and started to tell me how he was going to make it all up to me. I looked at him in complete awe. I told him that there was no way he could make this up to me. After I dropped him off, I went home and went to sleep for a few hours before I had to get up for work. I woke up to a dozen calls and texts from Ja'Kir apologizing for what he had done. He explained that not having his brother around for the holidays hurt, so he didn't want to be around his family. I accepted his apology and understood his pain. In the back of my mind, I couldn't help but think, "Well why the heck did you leave me over there for so long?" Nothing added up, but I took the high road and decided to be a good girlfriend. I was so in love with a compulsive liar, and I knew it.

Two weeks after Thanksgiving, he texted me and told me he was laid off his job. I didn't have the energy to sort through another lie he would come up with, so I just offered to help him get another job somewhere else. When I asked him to send me his resume, he claimed he could not find it on his computer. You would think since he worked with computers, finding his resume would be no issue. Weeks went by, and the man still couldn't produce a resume.

Finally, I created a plan to see if he would finally confess to never having a job on Wall Street in the first place. I found a position with a starting salary of 60k. Anyone seriously looking for work would have sent their resume with a quickness, not Ja'Kir. So I confronted him.

"What's the deal, Ja'Kir?" I asked. "I feel like you are lying just like you have about everything else."

He got offended and went ghost for days. I didn't care. He didn't say anything to me, and I didn't reach out to him. When he finally came back around, he acted as if nothing had happened. I made a mental note never to bring up the job again.

A few months later, he told me he got a new job with a moving company. I was proud of him and actually believed that he had a job. I did not question him. I just assured him that I believed him and would back him up 100%. As he went on and on about not wanting to wear a uniform after he had worked in suits for so long, a thought crossed my mind. It was strange that a computer programmer with eight years of experience on Wall Street had to settle for a job as a mover. Again, I didn't push this issue. I just shared in his excitement about his new J-O-B.

One evening, we drove to another cousin's house I never met. As usual, he left me and went to do God knows what. His cousin began to talk about stuff that had happened with Ja'Kir that I had no idea about. I confronted Ja'Kir about it, and of course, he had no idea what his cousin was talking about. At this point, I was really getting tired of Ja'Kir. I knew our time was slowly coming to an end. I knew that I would have to leave him. I didn't know how, but I knew the opportunity would present itself soon.

On Valentine's Day, Ja'Kir called me and asked me to come to his house to pick up my gift before he went to work. He came downstairs in regular clothes. He wasn't dressed in his work uniform, but I didn't care. I was excited to get my gift. He had some cheap balloons in his hand, so I just assumed my gift was in his pocket. I got out of the car, he handed me the balloons, kissed me on the cheek, and told me we would have dinner tomorrow. The day after Valentine's. I was livid. If this wasn't proof that he was seeing someone else, I don't know what else was. I was hurt, but I shrugged it off and went to work. I was slowly coming to the end of my rope with Ja'Kir.

His birthday rolled around, and I planned to do everything I could to make his day special. The man loved basketball, so I surprised him with tickets to the Knicks game. I took him to two lovely dinners and got him a very nice watch. After his birthday, he stopped calling and texting me as much. I was beyond confused.

I Finally Ran

Well one day, something told me to search for Ja'Kir on Facebook. He previously told me that he didn't have a Facebook page. I never thought to look before, but that day I did. After some heavy investigating, I found out that he had two Facebook pages. One was Ja'Kel Shoulders and the other Ja'Kir Shoulders. The Ja'Kel Shoulders profile stated that he was a computer programmer, 31 years old, and all this great information. The Ja'Kir Shoulders profile had his real age, and I noticed a picture of a little boy who had Ja'Kir's full name. The little boy was a Jr, so I realized that Ja'Kir had a son. I began to recall hearing his family talk about a Jr. several times. I asked Ja'Kir on three different occasions if he had a son. Each time, he said no. Also, on his Ja'Kel page, I saw many people wishing him a happy birthday. Most of the people were women. My pettiness got the best of me, and I wrote a Happy Birthday message on his page accompanied by a picture of the two of us cozied up at the Knicks basketball game.

In the meantime, my coworker and I monitored the page to see if any of the women would respond. As we waited, I took pictures of the pages and printed everything. A few hours later, the Ja'Kel Smith page disappeared.

I called Ja'Kir and asked if he could meet me in Brooklyn to go with me to my doctor's appointment. I had every intention of confronting him about everything, and I needed him to be in Brooklyn away from any trains just in case the argument turned bad and he wanted to take the train and leave. He met me at my job, we got in the car, and I headed towards the Canarsie Seaview Park in Brooklyn. On the way to the park, I asked him about the Facebook page, he immediately lied and reminded me that he didn't have a Facebook page. He asked about my doctor's appointment, and I told him I lied to get him out here since he'd been avoiding me. We finally got to the park, and I asked him about his son one last time. He started to get frustrated with me, so I pulled out every piece of paper I had with evidence that stated that he was a big-time liar. You think that changed anything? No. He lied even more. He never admitted to his son, or anything else. I was so done with that man, that I left him right there in the park and went home. I prayed, cried, and realized that I could not be with him any longer.

Weeks passed by, and I did not hear from Ja'Kir. One day while I was at work, he called me randomly as if we were on good terms. I was dry with him, and a few hours later, he showed up requesting to use my car. I denied his request, he cursed me out and left. Little did he know, my grandfather had just passed away, and I was in no mood for dealing with his nonsense. I sent a text telling him that my grandfather had died. His response was, "Okay. Are you going to let me use the car? I have things to do." That was the last and final straw for me. I never spoke to Ja'Kir again.

RED FLAGS RUN

I can't think of anyone who enjoys being with a liar. That's just uncommon. So, why are there so many women who fall for liars? Are they really that hard to detect? No, not at all.

When you first meet anyone, you must understand that you are meeting their representative. Everyone has a representative. Their representative is the personality of who they really want to be. Just think, most women want to give off the impression that they are cool with their man hanging out with the fellas, but weeks into the relationship, it suddenly becomes an issue. Did she change her mind? No, she just got tired of letting her representative run the show.

Before you get all crazy in love, give men the chance to get tired of being their representatives. After the honey moon stage, the truth will come out.

Even if someone seems to be upfront and telling the truth, give them time to show you who they actually are. Sometimes, we get into relationships and we fall hard and fast. By the time we look up, we're so deep in love that we don't know how to walk away even after our trust has been tainted.

When the next guy comes in your life, give him the time to be real in front of you. Don't just hang on to every word he says. Actually take the time to watch his actions and his character.

THE BROKE MAN

NAME: Courtney
LOCATION: Kansas City, MO
AGE: 27
OCCUPATION: Amazon/Semi-Pro Football Player
DEPENDENTS: 1
LENGTH OF RELATIONSHIP: 3 months

I travel to Kansas City often, around five times a year if not more. During one of my visits, I bumped into this sexy, dark-skinned, dread head, fit brother. We physically bumped into each other as we were walking out of a building. As he apologized for bumping me, my eyes just admired him. I really didn't hear a word he said. He was physically fit and real eye candy, if you know what I mean. Then, I snapped back to reality and realized where I was. I was in Kansas City, and I had this notion that everyone there was my cousin or something. Before I even accepted his apology, I blurted out, "Are we related?"

He laughed, "No, but can I get to know you?"

His smile was just as sexy as he was, so I gave him my number the minute he asked for it. I didn't want to seem thirsty or anything, but the man was fine. We talked briefly. I told him that I didn't live in Kansas, but I visited the area often. He expressed that distance wasn't an issue, and he was excited to get to know me. At first, we just texted then we upgraded our communication and started talking on the phone.

During our first conversation, he told me bluntly, "Listen, Ashley. I am looking for my wife, and I believe you are my wife. If you are not looking to get married, then please don't waste my time." I was taken aback, but I couldn't help but appreciate that he was a man who knew what he wanted. I didn't make any promises, but I told him my goal was to be married, and that I was interested in seeing where things would go with us. I wanted to be honest with him as well, so I opened up to him about all the issues I'd gone through with men using me for money, and treating me like crap. He was appalled that I had experienced so much turmoil and reassured me that I would never experience that kind of stuff again.

The first month or so was wonderful. He called to check in with me at least three times a day. I found out so many amazing things about him. He went to church every Sunday and always wanted to make sure I went as well. After church, he would share what his preacher taught, and how it changed his life. As time went on, he became even more intentional about calling me throughout the day. He would call on his way to work, during his break, on his way home to practice, after practice, etc. He spoiled me with attention, and I was falling for him hard and fast. Luckily, I wasn't falling alone. He soon expressed that he had fallen in love with me.

Red Flags

We got real comfortable with each other, and I noticed that Courtney began to ask me a lot of personal questions about my finances. At first, I was a little uncomfortable, but once I thought about it, it made sense. Any man really looking for a wife would naturally be concerned about her financial stability. I answered his questions about how much I made, my savings, and other investments. I'll be honest; I didn't tell him the whole truth because I was really concerned about him asking me for money later on. I shook off my apprehensions. I believed in my heart that he wouldn't do that.

We had barely made one month when he called me saying he needed financial assistance. I was on my way home from work, and he called me upset about the situation with his son's mother. He dogged his son's mother every chance he got. He said that she wouldn't allow him to see his son because of her new husband. Over the last few days, he had told me he was taking her to court to get custody of his son. I was careful not to join in with his baby-mama-bashing because I knew that there were always two sides to every story. Besides, I felt that if she was keeping him away from his son, there had to be a good reason. So anyway, this particular day, he explained that he needed $260 to pay for lawyer fees. When he asked me to help, I immediately shouted, "No!" I had promised myself that I would not allow another man to use me for money, and I was sticking to it.

"Baby, if I don't send this money in, my lawyer won't respond to me, and I won't have a chance to fight for custody of my son for months. I know what you've been through, but that's not me. I'm a hardworking man, but I get paid month to month. I just don't have it right now. Will you please help me?" he begged.

"I can't do it," I responded. "I'm sorry."

"Ashley, how are we going to be married if you can't hold me down in hard times? I thought you wanted to be my wife?" He said, "I would do the same thing for you. If it makes you feel better, I'll pay you back on my payday."

I kept refusing, but he kept pushing me until I was at the Western Union sending him the money. Yes, I fell for it. He was going to be my husband, so I figured I might as well get into the practice of sharing with him. I hated that I sent it to him, and I knew I wouldn't get the money back. After he picked up the money, things were back to normal, and he was back to loving me. I forgot about it and felt somewhat better.

From then on, every chance he got he would ask me for money. If I said no, he would go hard like a car salesman and would not let up until I was at the check cashing place or online sending his butt some money. If I said I didn't have any money, he would remind me about my savings account and my credit cards. If I put my foot down too hard, he would say, "Look, if you are not trying to help me out just let me know. I need a strong woman who can hold it down when I'm not able to. Remember, I will be in the NFL shortly signing a five-million-dollar contract. We are going to be good, Ashley. I just need you to stick this out with me." Each time, I would comply. Other than the money, he appeared to be a great man. I didn't want to lose him. Courtney didn't have a bank account, so I had to pay money to send money via Western Union. It cost me so much to send him the amounts he requested.

Around the end of our second month together, I went to Kansas City for a week. During that week, I took him to meet my family. He made such a great impression on my family. While I was there, I never saw where he lived. He only came over to my cousin's house to see me. He enjoyed the BBQ and home cooking so much that he called them to request dishes when I was gone back to NY. During my entire visit, he didn't offer to take me out or anything. He just enjoyed the free food and family time. He did, however, make it a point to ask me for gas money.

The Saturday before I got ready to leave, he had a semi-pro football game. I was excited to see him play. It was also the first time since I'd been there that we spent alone time together. Unfortunately, he twisted his ankle during the game. I felt bad for him. He was in a lot of pain. After the game, we went out for a drive, and he started to talk about how he needed to get money for a new car. I didn't say a word. I just listened. I knew where the conversation was headed. He stated that he would borrow money from a few of his friends to purchase his new car. He looked at me for feedback, but I refused to entertain the conversation one bit. I just let him talk. I could tell he got irritated with me. He got quiet and then mumbled something about wanting to go home because his ankle was hurting. He dropped me off at my cousin's, and I never saw him again during the rest of my stay. He claimed his ankle hurt too bad to go out. He said he went to the emergency room and they told him to stay off his ankle for a few days.

More Red Flags

When I returned to NY, the phone calls went from 10 times a day to once a week. I thought it was strange, but I figured he was busy resting, so I didn't bother bringing up his distance.

One day, he called and said, "We need to talk."

"Sure," I responded. "What's up?"

"Ashley, what you did was messed up," he began. "I told you I was having issues trying to get a new car and you didn't say a word."

"Well, what did you expect me to say?" I asked. " I didn't have the money to help you, so I just listened to you."

"You were supposed to step up, Ashley!" he exclaimed. "You are my woman! You should have shut it down the minute I said that I would have to go to friends for help. I shouldn't have to go to friends. I should be able to come directly to you!"

"Courtney, I just told you that I didn't have the extra money to help," I tried to explain before he cut me off.

"No, I know what it is Ashley. You just want to be with me because of my deal with the NFL. You're not really about me." He began to cry.

"That's not true, and you know it, Courtney!" I began to get upset.

"You don't! Here I am home with a messed up ankle. I can't work. I'm in pain. You are fine making plenty of money and won't even help me out. They don't pay us much out here. The price of living is so low, so I don't make enough right now. I'm just doing the best I can until this NFL contract comes through. All I want from you is just to hold me down. Is that too much to ask? Do you really want this, Ashley? Do you?" He continued to cry.

Needless to say, I felt horrible. I didn't have the money, but I did want to help him. We got off the phone, and I had a reality check with myself.

I asked him, "If the price of living is so low, then what are you spending your money on? I'm sure Amazon pays well."

He finally admitted that he never had money because he never had a job with Amazon. The only thing he was honest about was playing Semi-Pro football. I later found out that the NFL contract was a lie as well. He had never positioned himself to be picked up and recognized by a recruiter or agent. He was too busy trying to get over on me until he got hurt. After the constant arguments about money, and me finally having the courage to refuse to send him money, we broke up.

I Finally Ran

After the break-up, he would pop up every now and then to try to get me back. I always refused, and he went away for a while before returning to his same old games. Well around his birthday month, he got real persistent. So I took him back.

As his birthday approached, he called me wondering what I had up my sleeve for his birthday. I honestly hadn't thought about it since we had been broken up for so long. He expressed that he needed me to hook his birthday up. He had been down about his injury and really needed to get his mind right and have fun.

"Don't worry, baby," he said. "Your birthday is coming up next, and it is going to be crazy! I love you so much, and I've been saving up for your special day! I usually don't celebrate birthdays, but having you in my life changed all that. I'm so glad that we will be able to spoil each other on our birthdays."

Once again, I fell for it. The thought of really having a man to celebrate my special day at his expense excited me. So I made it my business to do something special for him. I got him a rental car so that he and his boys could drive to St. Louis, and I also sent money for him to spend on his special day. Before I sent the money, he asked me how much I would send.

"About $150," I said. I really didn't have an idea of how much I would send, but I just gave him a ballpark figure. He was disgusted with my response.

"Wow! How could you say that after what we've been through? I expected you to send at least $500 because it's my birthday. Baby that's low. Don't forget, I am going in for yours next month."

At that moment, my love for him slowly turned into hate. I still sent the money. When he got to St. Louis, he never called me. On the day of his birthday, I sent him a whole three-page letter about how amazing he was and a flip-a-gram with pictures and music. He never responded. I called him numerous times, and when he finally answered, he quickly told me that he was trying to enjoy his birthday, but I was ruining it with all the calls.

After his birthday, he finally called me.

"You know, Ashley, we haven't seen eye to eye lately. All the arguing we have been doing has been stressing me out. I need to be by myself." He said.

How convenient, I thought to myself. My birthday was weeks away, and he wanted to break up with me.

My birthday came and went, and he didn't even send me a text to say happy birthday. However, a few days after my birthday, he texted me saying he was stressed out and needed money for gas.

I was fed up with his crap, so I told him I would send the money and asked how much he needed. He responded that he only needed about $50. I told him I would send him $150 and he was blown away. I sent that joker a fake western union number, blocked his calls, and waited. I wish I were there to see the stupid look on his little arrogant face when he went to collect his "MONEY." When he did, he was livid. Since he couldn't call because I blocked him, he texted me several times. His texts ranged from, "That was messed up, Ashley," to "You should have been a real woman and told me that you didn't have any money!" He swore up and down never to call me again which was a lie.

I know you are probably getting tired of me talking about this guy, but months later, he had the nerve to reach out to one of my relatives. Courtney confronted him about no longer reaching out to him. He felt that just because we broke up didn't mean that they couldn't keep in touch with him or invite him over for family dinners and functions. Mind you, we were only in a relationship for three short months. That did not give him the clearance to keep in touch with my family, let alone eat at their houses. Well, that situation went from bad to worse. After that entire ordeal, I shut him off completely. He said some pretty ugly things to me, and I felt horrible. No matter what he said or did, I refused to send him money or even get back into the relationship.

RED FLAGS RUN

Being used hurts. Even though I was constantly being used for financial reasons, there are many other reasons why people are sometimes used in relationships. Some people are used for emotional support, sex, some are used just for company, the list goes on.

Look at the warning signs in the very beginning and pinpoint what you are being used for! When you see the red flags, don't second guess it. As for me and my experience, I knew in what areas I fell weak with men. It was always money! You saw this throughout every story I shared. Even though the men's issues varied, me giving of myself financially had always been an issue. It's easy to point out the flaws of others, but in order to grow, we must find the flaws of ourselves. When I realized where I was flawed, I was able to pinpoint where I was being used and why!

What are your weakness? Do you see yourself folding in these areas in every relationship? As you work on yourself, take note of your weaknesses, and be sure not to allow anyone to take advantage of these areas!

PART TWO

RED FLAGS IN DATING

THE DEACON

NAME: Shaheem

LOCATION: Brooklyn, NY

AGE: 29

OCCUPATION: Moving Company, Christian Rapper, Deacon

DEPENDENTS: 2

Shaheem (or Sha) and I were originally introduced by a mutual friend. When I met him, he was a very cool man. We hit it off immediately, exchanged numbers, and began having daily communication. After our initial visit, he came to my house. We sat in his car and talked about everything imaginable. We discussed the things we wanted out of life, marriage, kids, careers, and Christianity. At the time, I was not heavy in my faith, but he was. This man was a card-carrying deacon, and he was proud of it. His faith drew me to him more than anything else. I admired that he was a faithful servant of God.

We sat in the car for so long that I got hungry! He said that he was as well, so we decided to drive to Long Island to eat at a place called Bronx BBQs. He was driving a "hoopty" that had seen better days. So, he asked me to drive. I gladly said yes. With the condition that car was in, I wouldn't have ridden with him anyway. He assured me that he only used the car for work and that he had a Range Rover parked at his condo.

We had an amazing time at the restaurant. He was very funny, and we both made each other laugh. When the bill came, Sha just continued to talk, and I followed suit. Ten minutes had gone by, and he still had not touched the bill.

"Whew, that was good," I said. "I guess we should go now."

"Yeah, let's get out of here. Hurry up and pay the bill so we can go!" he replied.

"Excuse me?" I asked. I wanted to make sure I heard him properly.

"You invited me to dinner," he explained. "So that means you have to pay."

I looked at him like he was crazy. Part of me wanted to pay for my portion, jet out of there, and leave his dusty behind sitting where he was. Once I saw that he was serious, I paid for the meal. I didn't want to create a scene. I made a mental note that I would not be seeing this guy again.

As we were headed to the car, he suggested that we see a movie. I gave him the nastiest look. He laughed and assured me that it would be his treat. Once we got in the theater, I suggested two movies, and he shut both of them down. He claimed he didn't see anything he wanted to watch, so we left. Our car ride was very quiet, and I drove as fast as I could. I wanted that cheap man out of my car as soon as possible. When we got home, I ran for the door, but he grabbed my hand and pulled me close for a hug.

"I really enjoyed you," he said with a smile.
I bet you did, I thought. I gave him a weak smile and told him to have a good night. An hour hadn't passed by, and Sha was calling my phone. He wanted to let me know how much fun he had, and how he could see me as his wife. I rolled my eyes

and responded dryly. If that wasn't enough, the man asked to take me out on a second date. I got clarity on who would be paying the bill before I agreed. He assured me that it would be his treat. He even had the nerve to laugh as if I wasn't asking a legitimate question.

We decided to go to dinner after church the following Sunday. That morning, he told me to call him when I got out of church. I thought it was strange that "The Deacon" wasn't at church, but I didn't concern myself with it. After church, he texted me the address to his condo for me to pick him up. I thought surely we would be driving the Range Rover that beautiful Sunday evening, but he claimed his brother was borrowing it.

So I pulled up, and before I could park, he was running into the car. He was looking over his shoulder as if someone was following him. He seemed real paranoid and sort of rushed me out of the driveway. Once we were clear of his condo, he asked me where I wanted to go. I told him about a soul food spot I wanted to try called Aunt Sophia's. I drove to Aunt Sophia's, and we sat down to eat and talk. The place was not expensive at all to my surprise. Each of our meals came up to $11, and the drinks were about $2 each.

When the bill came, he screamed, "Well damn! What did she get?"

Everyone around us looked at him and shook their head in disbelief. I could not believe he made a big deal out of a $28 bill when the other day he had steak and lobster on me. "Look," I said very quietly. "I'll take care of my portion of the bill."

"No, I got it," he pouted. As he paid the bill, he mumbled something under his breath about me picking an expensive and fancy restaurant. Once he was finished acting like a little kid, we got in my car and left. Instead of pulling into his condo, he asked me to drop him off close to the road. I thought that was weird, but I didn't even have a desire to find out why.

Later, he invited me to see him perform one of his gospel rap songs at a youth concert. I heard a few of his songs before on YouTube, and I was delighted to see him do his thing. The day of the event, he called me very upset to tell me the program had been canceled, until further notice. He sounded sad and disappointed. He didn't seem to want to share the details, so I didn't press the issue. We talked for a brief moment before he rushed off the phone to do something.

The day after, I was at my friend's Stacie house hanging out. He called me and said he needed a hug. I told him I wasn't at home, but he was persistent and said he would come wherever I was. After I got permission from Stacie, Sha came over. I introduced him to Stacie, and we went on the porch to chat. While we were talking, Stacie had this bright idea to do a double date. She was married and thought it would be cool for us to go out for dinner and a movie. Sha and I agreed.

On the day of our double date, it rained hard. I thought Sha would cancel. To my surprise, he called and told me he would be done at the studio in fifteen minutes, and needed me to pick him up. The studio was about seven minutes from my house, so I agreed to pick him up. I finished getting dressed and waited for him to call me and say he was ready to go. After all, the studio wasn't that far away, and I was in no rush to go out into the rain.

Sha called me about five minutes later to ask what my status was. When I told him I was walking out of the door, he flipped out on me. He was upset that I was not in the car on my way to pick him up.

"Are you serious, Ashley?" he yelled. "I am outside stuck in the rain without an umbrella! Hurry up and get here."

"Woah," I said, "Pump your brakes. You never mentioned being stranded outside without an umbrella. You need to lower your voice and have some respect."

"Whatever. Just hurry up," he said and hung up the phone.

I rolled my eyes. At this point, I no longer wanted to go anywhere with him, but I didn't want to let my friend down. She was so excited about our double date. When I finally pulled up to the pitiful looking Sha, I actually started to feel bad for him. That is until he got in the car, took one look at me, and immediately began cursing me out. I could not believe the words that came out of his mouth. I could not believe that a card-carrying deacon could be so mean! He ranted about how my shirt was inappropriate and that I needed to change it immediately. I thought I looked great. I was wearing one of those sheer cute tops, but nothing was hanging out or showing. It wasn't even a low-cut. He complained the entire ride to Stacie's house, and I finally parked the car to go inside. I went in and asked Stacie for a different shirt. She was confused, but she gave me the shirt. I explained to her that I wanted to keep the peace with Sha, and she immediately got upset. I told Stacie it was okay, changed my shirt, and we all got in one car so we could ride together.

Once we got to the restaurant, her husband, Alfred, drove Stacie and me to the door so we wouldn't get wet. Would you believe that Sha jumped out of the car as well? I was immediately annoyed and embarrassed. We got in the restaurant, sat down, and Alfred went to wash his hands. Stacie said to Sha playfully, "Don't get no attitude with my friend for her shirt, or I will beat you up." Granted she shouldn't have said anything, but she was honestly playing. Well, Sha took it seriously and shut completely down. He didn't say one word at the dinner. I was mortified. During dinner, I noticed him trying to get the waitress' attention, so I decided to call her myself.

"I don't need your help with anything. I got it!" Sha yelled as he rolled his eyes and told the lady he wanted some sauce for his shrimp. I could tell Stacie and Alfred were very uncomfortable with the way Sha acted towards me. When Sha got up from the table to go to the bathroom, Alfred said, "Yea, I don't want to see you with this clown again."

Finally, the bill came, and Sha didn't even grab the bill to see how much it cost. He threw $13 on the table for his meal and headed to the door. That was the last straw. If Alfred hadn't already bought all of our tickets, I would have ended the date right then. The movie theater was right across the street from the restaurant, so we all just walked over. Sha walked alone as if he wasn't even with us. I walked up to him and said quietly, but sternly, "Aye, son. You can go home! You don't have to see the movie. You didn't pay for it anyway! I will gladly give your ticket to one of these strangers. Try me." He looked at me for a minute, humbled himself, got his ticket, and walked away. He finally came and sat by me, but he acted as if I had a skin disease the entire time. He went so far as to huff and puff each time I brushed against him. Once the movie was over, Alfred went to get the car, and Sha stayed with us like a girl waiting for Alfred to bring the car around. In the car, only the three of us talked, and Sha looked out the window with an attitude. When we made it back to my car, I took him home and sped off before he even got a chance to say anything. I vowed to never speak to that weirdo ever again. Before I went to bed that night, I blocked his number to make sure he wouldn't be able to call me again.

RED FLAGS RUN

Are you ready to point out the red flags? Use the space below to point out the red flags you found in this dating fiasco!

_____

_____

_____

_____

_____

_____

_____

_____

_____

_____

THE CONVICT

NAME: Mario

LOCATION: Newark, NJ

AGE: 32

OCCUPATION: Flower Delivery Company

DEPENDENTS: None

It was a cold day in January when I met Mario. I was driving down Church Avenue in Brooklyn, NY when he flagged me down at a traffic light. He asked me to pull over somewhere because he wanted to get to know me. Crazily enough, I did. What can I say? I was a very adventurous girl, and I believed that love could find me in the craziest places. I pulled over, and when he got out the car, I thought he was very handsome. He had dreads, and he was dressed very nice. He sealed the deal when he opened his mouth, and this deep, sexy voice drawled out. He honestly had me at hello. The cologne he wore would make any woman weak. After we had exchanged numbers, it was hard to drive away from him. I wanted to hang out with him right then and there, but I couldn't be thirsty. So, I drove off and waited for him to call me first. Later that day, he did. We talked for awhile and found out that we had a lot in common.

We talked for a few weeks back and forth before we finally decided to go on our first date. The day I met him, he told me he didn't live in NY, he was just there for business. So, I drove my little Nissan Sentra out to meet him in New Jersey for our first date. It was a 40-minute drive, but I did not mind. I met him at what he said was his brother's house. I parked my car, and we drove his car to a movie and dine theater somewhere in New Jersey.

We got to the movies, walked to the register, and to my surprise, he did not give me the famous I lost my wallet line. He pulled out an extremely large wad of cash and paid for our tickets. Everyone around us saw him whip out the money and stared. He was a black man with a wad of cash, so I knew what they were thinking. I looked at them and smiled politely. I stood confidently next to that fine man and walked into the movies on his arm. Once the movie was over, he drove us back to my car so that I could head back to Brooklyn. Before I left, I realized that I didn't have any cash for the tolls, so I asked him where the nearest ATM was. Even though I knew he had it, I refused to ask him for money. He got in his car and told me to follow him to the nearest gas station. When we arrived at the gas station, we both went inside. He noticed someone there he knew and proceeded to have a full-fledged conversation with them. I got my cash and was ready to get back home due to work the next morning. I didn't want to seem rude, but I really didn't want to get home late. I also didn't want to take off without saying goodbye. After all, we had a great date, and he cared enough to make sure I got to the gas station safely. Once he came out the store, we hugged, and I left. I got home very fast and sent him a quick text saying to let him know I made it home. I never received a response from him, so I just assumed he fell asleep.

The next few days we texted. He had enjoyed our date and looked forward to our next one. Our schedules conflicted, and I could not make it out to New Jersey until the following week. I asked him to come to New York, but he said he couldn't. Apparently, he had several meetings for the flower delivery company he owned. I googled the company name and found it, but I didn't find a website listing him as the owner or anything.

Two weeks later, I reached out to Mario but never heard back. I called him and sent numerous text messages to, but still got no response back. I wasn't that worried about him, but I was curious as to what he was up to. I put my friend/private investigator, Keisha, on the job. The girl was good. She could find any man whether he was in jail, living in another state with a secret family, or just down the block. Low and behold, Keisha found out he was in jail. We did not find out the exact reason, but as soon as he got out, he dialed my phone and apologized. He expressed how much he missed me and wanted to see me again. We didn't talk much about why he was locked up. He only said that it wasn't his fault.

I felt sorry for the brother, so I drove out to New Jersey once again to see him. This time, all we did was sit in his car and talk for about two hours. It was no date, just a night of talking outside in front of his home. He didn't even invite me into the house. I had to use the restroom, and the man suggested that we go to the nearest gas station. So I left, went home, and did not bother telling him I was home safe. The next day, I was at work and received a panic text from Mario to call him ASAP. I finally got away from my desk and gave him a call. He told me he lost $3000 and claimed it fell out of his pocket. All I could think was who walks around with $3000 in their back pocket like it's a pack of gum? He rambled on and on about him not being able to see his mother who was sick. He had been saving the money to rent a car and visit her in Virginia. The money was also to help her with some of the household bills. He went on and on about how he couldn't afford to rent a car and visit his mother. I knew that money was typically not an issue for him because of our first date, so I felt bad for him. I offered to pay for his rental car for the three days he would need it. I didn't want to do it, but I wanted to do something to help him get to his mother.

So the day came for him to get the rental car. I told him to meet me in New York, but he wanted to use a rental place in New Jersey because his friend worked there and could give him a deal. So I drove to New Jersey and waited almost an hour for Mario to pick me up. I was livid because I had to be at work in Manhattan in 20 minutes. He finally pulled up and drove us both to a Hertz rental car place in Jersey City, NJ.

When I got in the car, he was excited. He claimed his friend, Tony, would give him a discount of $50 per day, which was really good considering we were in New Jersey. When we got there, I gave Tony all of my info, and the entire deal was complete. Mario promised that the rental car would only be used for three days. He would see his mother and come right back. I went to work as if nothing happened and proceeded with my day.

I did not hear from Mario for the first two days he was away, and I got nervous. The third day arrived, and I still hadn't heard from Mario. I got nervous, so I checked my accounts. Everything was fine. So far, I had only been charged for two days. However, it was the third day, and Mario should have been making his way back. I called Tony at work and asked if he had heard from Mario. I also warned him that if Mario didn't call me with the status of the car, I would call the cops and report the rental stolen. After all, I did not have the rental car in my possession, and I had every right to call the cops. Mario received my message and called immediately. He was upset that I threatened to do such a thing. He was so disappointed in me for taking things as far as I did, but he said he would have it for one more day, then drop it off. I finally agreed. I checked my app and saw that I had been charged for a total of five days. By this time, I was livid. I called Mario, and he informed me that he had dropped the car off at the Newark airport. I went off on him about how that would incur an extra fee because we didn't pick it up there. He acted as though he didn't know that.

I was angry, but I was just glad that the car was out of his possession. I was finally at ease and stopped checking the app. The next month, my statement came, and I saw a $763.00 charge from the rental company. He had not dropped the car off when he said he would. He kept the car for a total of ten days. He stated that he would give me half of the money, but I would have to cover the rest. I was livid. When it was time for him to pay his part, he went ghost. When I called Mario's phone, it went straight to voicemail. I ended up having to pay the entire bill on my own.

Two weeks later, he called from another number claiming his phone was cut off and asked if I could buy him a T-Mobile card to turn his phone back on. I hung up the phone and never answered another one of his outrageous texts.

A few months later, I was in Pittsburgh for a wedding when I received a text message from my mother. She told me I received mail for a ticket I got in Washington, DC in a Hertz rental. I instantly became upset. One, she opened my mail, and two, I never rented a car from Hertz. The last time I was in Washington, DC I was in Junior High School on a school trip. I told her she was bugging and that I would look into it when I got back to NY. I continued to dance when suddenly it hit me. It was that fool, Mario. He had gotten a ticket, and since he didn't tell me, it incurred interest. By the time I got the ticket, it was $256.93. I wanted to find him and curse him out. I found his number and called him multiple times. When he answered and found out who I was, he hung up quickly. After that, my calls went straight to voicemail. This man left me with a credit card bill of $763.00 and months later I had an additional fee of $256.93. What can I say? Being stupid costs.

RED FLAGS RUN

Are you ready to point out the red flags? Use the space below to point out the red flags you found in this dating fiasco!

THE DIVA

NAME: Richard

LOCATION: Harlem, NY

AGE: 45

OCCUPATION: Personal Trainer

DEPENDENTS: 1

One day, my coworker, Jennifer encouraged me to work out with her. She was hosting a personal training session, and I was excited to go. My weight had always been a struggle for me, so I very was excited to try something different. When I got there, I waited in the lobby until I saw Jennifer. When Jennifer arrived, she introduced me to the trainer, Richard, who was also waiting in the lobby. After she had introduced us, she walked away for a moment. Richard looked me up and down for a moment and said, "Okay. Okay. I know just how to change your body into the way I like it." He was literally staring at me as if I was some kind of project. What a weirdo, I thought to myself.

"Umm. Okay. I guess," I replied.

Later, we went to the seaport, had a great workout, and split. We got each other's numbers strictly for possible workout sessions. Richard had given me such a weird first impression, that I honestly didn't want anything else from him.

Apparently, Jennifer had a remaining balance of nine dollars from the training, so she asked Richard to meet her at her church to give him the money. Richard had been to her church in the past and stated that he did not want to get shot, insinuating that Jennifer's church was in a bad neighborhood. They couldn't seem to find a place and time that worked for the two of them.

Days went by, and he began to call Jennifer and me numerous times wanting his nine dollars. I totally understood, however, it wasn't like Jennifer hadn't tried to get him the money. He made such a fuss about the nine bucks, and it was rather annoying. It had nothing to do with me, but he insisted on including me in the entire situation.

He later asked if he could be my personal trainer, and offered some payment plans. Because of the previous issues, I didn't want to deal with him. I ignored him and thought nothing of it.

Jennifer later informed me that Richard had been talking to her about me, and hinted that he wanted to pursue something with me. I wasn't interested, so when he called me, I refused to answer.

Five months after we met, I finally decided to go on a date with him, but I had my reservations. Our phone conversations were always so weird. He was very argumentative, and would sometimes ask me questions just to argue with my response. It aggravated the heck out of me. The man would argue about anything. He actually found joy in doing so.

Now, there was another young lady, Lauren, who was very close friends with Richard. He trained her as well. We worked for the same company, so it didn't take long for me to find out that she liked Richard. I'd also heard that he talked down to her, and belittled her quite often. Apparently, Richard began to tell the girl things about me. I'm not sure what he said to her, but it caused her to dislike me.

Richard had several qualities that I just didn't care for. One day, while I was in Kansas City visiting my family, he called me super excited. I thought the man had landed a major client or something, but that was not the case. Apparently, his church members went to Jennifer's church to support their pastor. He didn't go, of course, but everyone told him that there were more of his church members there than Jennifer's church family. He was stoked that his members outnumbered Jennifer's members in their own church. I was utterly disgusted. His church was way larger than Jennifer's church, so I didn't understand why he was surprised, or why it even mattered. Never the less, I hit him with my famous, "I'll call you back," and never did.

He realized he had rubbed me the wrong way, and called back later to chat.

"Ashley, we've been knowing each other long enough," he said. "It's time for us to go on a date." I was not interested, but I told him I would go on a date with him when I got back to NY. Once I got home, he called me and hinted at what I promised, but I never committed to a date. Weeks passed by before I finally agreed to let him take me out one day after church.

His means of transportation was the NYC transit, which was cool. Living in NY is expensive, so most people don't have cars. Honestly, we don't need cars because of our many transportation options. After church, I drove over to pick him up from his church. I parked and waited for him to come outside. As I waited, I noticed a man on a bike who looked exactly like Richard's pastor. When Richard hopped in the car, I told him what I saw, and he immediately shut me down. "That could never be my pastor," he said. "My pastor would never be on a bike around this area." He was clearly offended, so I apologized and changed the subject.

He quickly asked how my service went, but before I could finish a full sentence, he interrupted me to tell me how excited he was about getting to use the special restroom at his church. According to him, the restroom was only to be used by pastors and special guests. He felt so important and couldn't stop raving about his experience. The more he talked, the more I regretted agreeing to go on a date with him.

127

As we drove, I made restaurant suggestions in Brooklyn, and he turned his nose up at each of them. Finally, he requested that I drive out to Long Island. Mind you, the restaurants I suggested were only seven minutes away from where his church was located. They were great spots, but he just refused to stay in Brooklyn. When we got to Long Island, we pulled into a Red Lobster, and it was packed. I asked him to go in and check on the wait time, but he refused to get out of the car. He felt like it would be a waste of his time, so we left. After driving around for hours, he pointed out an Applebees and requested that we dined there. We had passed hundreds of Applebees, but he just had to have this one. He refused to dine anywhere else. The man acted like a straight diva.

We walked in and waited to be seated. Seconds after we had been seated, he began to ask a long list of questions.

"What exactly do you do at church?" he asked.

"I am a Praise and Worship leader," I responded. "I also teach dance or sometimes dance myself."

"Oh no," he replied. "If you are going to be my woman, you will need to do more in ministry." I just stared at him.

"What do you do for fun?" he asked next.

"I hang out with family, travel, read, shop, and go to amusement parks. That sort of thing. What about you?" I was anxious to know something about him since he was just so judgmental of everyone else.

He stared at me for a minute. "You are boring," he replied. "That's not fun. Fun is getting on a plane to Florida for the day to go to an amusement park. I'm clearly going to have to teach you how to have a good time. You are going to be a lot of work for me." I couldn't believe the words that came out that fool's mouth. What a dummy, I thought to myself. I wanted to get in my car and leave that diva right there.

"I am going to start a great church someday," he announced to me.

"Oh, that's great. When?" I asked.

"I don't plan on leaving my church until my pastor really recognizes me," he responded. Now, in previous phone conversations, he had spoken highly of his pastor as if they were best buds. So, I didn't understand what he meant.

"What do you mean?" I asked. I was very concerned.

"My pastor doesn't know me," he responded. It took everything in me not to burst out laughing. The man was clearly delusional. An hour ago, he almost wanted to fight me for thinking his pastor was on a bike. The man didn't even know he existed! Anyway, most of our conversation consisted of him gossiping and talking about people. I was highly disgusted. Every time he got excited, he would say "YASSSSSSSS," just like a girl. To make matters worse, I just had to open my big mouth and tell him that my father was a Senior Pastor. His eyes lit up like a child on Christmas morning. I had clearly put the cherry on top of his imaginary sundae.

"Yaassss!" he shouted. "I have to search for your father on Google. This changes the whole dynamic of our relationship! I need to know everything about your dad and his ministry. Who knows, I might just bless your church with a good sermon one day. When we get married, you will have to leave your daddy's church and come to mine, so don't get too comfortable over there!" He went on and on. The man talked a mile a minute and didn't pause for me to respond. In a matter of minutes, he had our entire lives planned out. Meanwhile, I was still trying to figure out when we got in a relationship.

The waiter asked if we wanted dessert, and I shouted no so fast, I think I scared the poor guy. I just wanted the date from hell to end. When we got in the car, I rushed to get him back to Brooklyn. I never drove so fast in my life! If he had shouted, "Yassssss" one more time, I would have thrown his fit butt out on the streets without even stopping the car. We finally got into Brooklyn, and he asked me to drop him off at a nearby McDonald's where his friends were hanging out. I didn't ask any questions. I just took him there. When we got to McDonald's, he motioned for me to get out of the car and give him a hug. Just as the hug ended, he kissed me on my lips, and I almost vomited. When I got in my car, I wiped my lips like a crazy lady. When I got home, I jumped in the shower and scrubbed my lips even more. I didn't want any trace of that annoying diva.

Instead of telling him that we would not work out, I simply blocked his number. I guess he eventually got the message because word got around that he was gossiping about me to Jennifer and Lauren. Being the diva that he was, I expected nothing more of him.

Since he couldn't get a reaction out of me, he began to make subliminal Facebook statuses aimed at me. He even went so far as to inbox me. I just ignored him. Everything in me wanted to blast that diva on social media, but I kept my cool and ignored him.

Months later, he messaged me and asked me for my new number. I told him, no, and he replied, "I hope you don't think you are all that, cause you are not! I was trying to give you a chance to be with greatness, but you have lost it. You don't have to worry about me trying to help you ever again."

I simply responded, "Yaaaasssssss!"

RED FLAGS RUN

Are you ready to point out the red flags? Use the space below to point out the red flags you found in this dating fiasco!

_____

_____

_____

_____

_____

_____

_____

_____

_____

_____

THE MUTE

NAME: Terrance aka TK

LOCATION: Queens, NY

AGE: 40

OCCUPATION: Cellphone Tech

DEPENDENTS: None

My dad was performing at a wedding, and since I knew the groom, I decided to go. Once I arrived, I looked around for my family. My sister was in town for the wedding as well. After I found my family, I went over to congratulate the groom. I wanted to be polite and introduce myself to the bride before I spoke to her groom. I walked up to her and said hello. I wasn't sure if she remembered me, so I let her know I was the pastor's daughter. She remembered who I was, we chatted briefly, and I turned to walk away. Just as I was turning around, this older man stepped up to me. Apparently, he had heard our conversation and proceeded to say, "You have your own identity, you know. You are a very beautiful woman." I smiled, said thanks, and quickly walked over to my sister and the bride's brother. So as I was telling them about what happened, the older gentleman was standing quietly behind me. I noticed that my sister was looking weird, so I turned around and noticed that the man was standing there the entire time. I was so embarrassed. We all laughed, and I soon learned that the man's name was Terrance. He was the bride's older brother. Everyone called him TK.

TK's brother and my sister began to talk about Terrance and I hooking up as if neither of us was standing there. TK and I just stood there silently as the two of them went back and forth about our great credentials and compatibility. Eventually, they exchanged our numbers for us. It was very awkward, to say the least.

The next day, I went to the groom's mother's house. Everyone was hanging out and eating when TK came strolling through the door. I was stunned at first, but then I smiled. We spoke then walked into the living room to chat. There were kids everywhere. Just as we turned to find a quieter place, my sister cleared out the living room loudly, looked at me, smiled, and walked away. I was so embarrassed, but I wasn't shocked.

My embarrassment didn't end there. TK told me that my sister had found him on Facebook and invited him over. I was mortified and immediately apologized on behalf of my sister's great stalking skills. He assured me that it was cool. After that, we barely talked. He was very quiet. There was no communication or chemistry. So I got up a few times to see what everyone else was doing. They all smiled at me and gave me that look. If they only knew the boredom that was on the other side of that wall, I thought to myself.

The next day, we all got together and went to a restaurant in downtown Brooklyn. My sister lived in Atlanta, so she wanted to see everyone before she left. Of course, she insisted that I invited TK. The entire night, he spoke quietly to his sister, sat by me, and didn't say very much. Very similar to the night before. When it was time to leave, my sister and aunt suggested that he drive me back home so that they could use my car to run an errand. We rode in complete silence. The only thing he said to me was, "Hey, we are here." It was so quiet that I hadn't noticed I had slept the entire ride. I opened my door, and he told me he enjoyed taking me home and asked when he would see me again. I told him we would figure it out, thanked him for the ride, and walked away.

As soon I got upstairs, my sister had a thousand questions. I immediately shut down the wedding she had planned in her head. I told her that TK and I had no chemistry. She went in on me. In her opinion, I always picked the wrong guy because I picked the thugs. She said that TK had a lot going for himself, so I should give him a try. I just kept quiet and agreed to give TK another shot.

I called him the next day. We greeted each other, shared how we were doing, and then the phone went silent. I pushed and pushed for a conversation, but it just wasn't happening on his part. He continued to call me, but the conversations were always the same. Four months went by, and we hadn't even gone on a date. I was ready to throw in the towel, so I called my sister and broke the news to her. She didn't believe me, so I told her I would three-way her into the call the next time TK called me. In less than a minute, TK was calling me. I quickly merged the call, and my sister put her phone on mute.

The conversation went exactly like this:

Me: Hey TK, what's up!

TK: Hey youuuuu (this was his signature line by the way.)

Me: So, What's up? What are you doing?

TK: I'm on my way to work, but you know that.

Me: Oh. Okay, I gotcha.

SILENCEEEE (for about 2 minutes)

Me: How is the weather outside now?

TK: I'm not a meteorologist

Me: Okay

SILENCEEEE (1 more minute)

TK: I know what you are trying to do.

(I was so scared. I thought he knew my sister was on the phone.)

Me: No, what are you talking about?

TK: You are trying to get me to talk. Aren't you?

Me: What? Let me call you right back.

I was so done with him. I clicked over to my sister. We cracked up for about five minutes. She completely understood and gave me clearance to shut down Mission Impossible.

Months later, he began to text and call me again. Surprisingly enough, he had a lot to say on the phone. It was really weird, but I didn't think anything of it. I talked to him, but always said I would call him back and never did. This continued for a month or so. Finally, one day he called and said, "Ashley, I am ready to fix whatever I need to fix to get us together." Here it was a whole year since we had met, and he was finally ready to date me. For weeks he pushed for a date, but I never gave him a direct answer. I figured he would fall off the wagon, but he was very persistent.

One day, we were on the phone, and he said he was ready for us to be a couple and that he was ready for a roommate. I shut the idea down and let him know that I would not be moving in with any man unless I was married. He responded by asking me what kind of ring I wanted.

It was a whole year since we met, he hadn't taken me on a date, but here he was talking about a ring. I realized that he was playing games, and I didn't have time for it. I wasn't really interested in him, so I sent him a nice text to end it all. Here's what I said:

So, here's the thing. I do not feel the need to pursue a relationship with you. We tried, and it didn't work out. I feel it happened that way for a reason. I'm in a totally different place in my life, and I don't have time for nonsense. I'm doing things God's way, and there is no room for error. You're still my homie, TK, but I'm not interested in a relationship with you.

He responded the next day, and we texted very briefly. I could tell he wanted me to change my mind about him, but I didn't budge.

Later that week, I remembered that he never gave me the number for a guy who knew how to fix treadmills, so I texted him. He gave me the number, but said nothing else. So I gave him a call to thank him. He dryly told me that it was no problem. It was clear that he didn't want to talk, so before I ended the call, I asked, "Hey, what does this guy call you?

Terrance or TK?" He lost his mind. He yelled and chastised me as if I was his child.

"Does that make any sense, Ashley? Really? Does that make any sense?" He yelled. "Do you hear yourself? Why would he call me TK?"

I was ready to hang up the phone on him, but I let him talk. I was in disbelief. He was clearly upset about my text. I had assumed that we were still cool enough to be cordial associates, but I was so wrong. After he had finished talking to me crazy, I hung up the phone, deleted his number, and just stared at the phone in disbelief.

The very next morning, I received a call from TK aka Mr. Disgusting Attitude. He called to apologize for lashing out at me. He explained that he was in a bad mood due to someone dying. When I asked him who died, he rambled something about a family member in Alabama. He rushed me off the phone before I could get any more details. That was the last time I spoke to him.

RED FLAGS RUN

Are you ready to point out the red flags? Use the space below to point out the red flags you found in this dating fiasco!

PART THREE

SELF REFLECTION

Red Flags Run

Now that you've read about the red flags in a few of my crazy relationships, let's take a look at your relationships! Pull out your journal and answer the following questions about your past relationships before you go on another date! If you are currently in a relationship, use these questions to determine if the relationship is worth another minute of your time!

Looking Back...

1. Did you notice any RED FLAGS on the first date or when you first talked on the phone? If so, what were they?

2. Did those RED FLAGS continue out in the relationship? If so, what made you stay?

3. How long did this relationship last?

4. What made you realize that it was time to leave?

5. What made you stay as long as you did?

6. What did you expect from the relationship?

7. What hurt you most about the relationship?

8. What did you learn from the relationship?

9. What are your relationship weaknesses?

10. Did you compromise any of your morals? If so, what were they, and why?

11. How will you ensure that you don't make the same mistakes in your next relationship?

Moving Forward....

1. What do you desire in a relationship?

2. What are your major desires?

3. What are you willing to compromise on?

STAY CONNECTED

Thank you for purchasing Red Flags Run. Ashley would like to stay connected with you! Below are a few ways you can stay updated on her new releases, speaking engagements, book signings, and more!

EMAIL redflagsrun@gmail.com

INSTAGRAM @ashleywgillett @redflagsrun

FACEBOOK Ashley W. Gillett and Red Flags Run

WEBSITE www.redflagsrun.com

Made in the USA
Middletown, DE
12 September 2017